Who Needs A Damn Therapist Anyway?

Who Needs A Damn Therapist Anyway?

A GUIDE TO BELIEVING IN YOURSELF

11-15-2015

Believe in Yourself in all.
You do. Enjoy your life with
hope and peace. Always

Cecilia
Tucker

Cecilia A. Tucker LMFT

ISBN: 0692431705
ISBN 13: 9780692431702
Library of Congress Control Number: 2015909505
Cecilia A. Tucker, St. Petersburg, FL

This book is dedicated to my clients, who for over thirty-five years and counting, have so aptly used these insights and skills to move through life *believing* in *your*selves.

Endorsements

"Cecilia's insight and direction took me to a place where healing could begin. She is patient, kind, and will kick you in the butt when you need it."
—*Melinda S. Kesson*

"I first met Cecilia [when I was] a child, and she immediately put me at ease with her humor and kindness. With her deep passion to help and genuine empathy, we connected on a profound level. I worked with Cecilia through my adolescence, and her ability to understand me and speak *to* me and *with* me taught me accountability and not to lay blame on external things or others for issues that lie within me. Working with Cecilia was not typical therapy; she brought peace to my confusion and troubles."
—*Amanda Fett*

"Cecilia is a no-nonsense, cut-to-the-chase type of person. Everybody should have a Cecilia in his or her life. She's unconventional—that's what makes her so effective. She doesn't just talk the talk since she's been through so many of her own trials. We are blessed to know her."
—*Chris Lewis*

"Cecilia is such a warm and unique person to work with. She has a down-to-earth approach that makes her easy to speak with. Her background as a minister also gave me a great deal of comfort. Cecilia is a true blessing to everyone she meets."
—*Danielle Banks*

Contents

Acknowledgments

Thanks to my family and friends for supporting me through this journey. Thanks to Kristin for helping to put my stories into readable book form. Thanks to Dr. Harold Wahking, my mentor, teacher, and door opener for my life's work as a therapist. And thanks be to God Almighty for allowing me to be a conduit of compassion and hope for others.

EGO STATES GOAL: A BALANCE OF ALL

Ego States at the start of the therapy journey

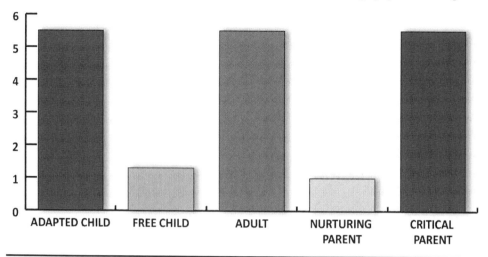

As the **Adapted Child (AC)**, we rebel, withdraw or comply because of what we were taught as a child.

As the **Critical Parent (CP)**, we live in the space of Should/Ought/Must/Never and Always.

Our **Adult State (AS)** keeps us centered and balanced between all stages, but it's so full of the myths we've been fed our entire lives, it keeps us ping-ponging between **AC** and **CP** most often.

We have moments when we allow ourselves to live in **Free Child (FC)**, where we are creative, spontaneous and don't care what others think, but it usually gets squashed by **AC** or **CP**.

We spend very little time in **Nurturing Parent (NP)** as well, being good to ourselves, encouraging, supporting and being open-minded to whom we really want to be, who we are deep inside. Again, the minute we feel confidence or think about being completely open, **AC** or **CP** come calling and remind us that people will judge or we "shouldn't because."

Most adults spend the majority of their lives living in the **Adapted Child (AC)** and **Critical Parent (CP)** worlds and very little time in **Free Child (FC)** and **Nurturing Parent (NP)**. At some point our childhood myths and messages catch up to us and we find ourselves seeking our inner-truth. We wear ourselves out living in the **AC** and **CP** states because we're constantly trying to figure out who we need to be for every person around us. Once we transfer that energy to **FC** and **NP** in our daily lives, dispel childhood myths and choose to live spontaneously, encouraging of our self and others, we end up thriving.

EGO STATES GOAL: A BALANCE OF ALL

Desired Ego States as growth occurs throughout and post-therapy

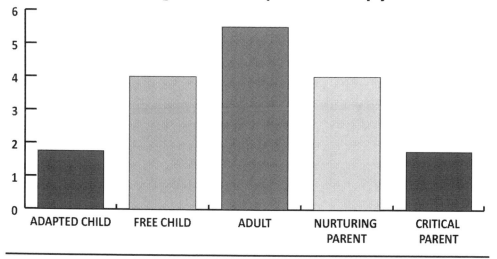

As you read this book and do the exercises, you will start to live less in **AC** and **CP**, allowing **Free Child** and **Nurturing Parent** to arise, all while the **Adult State** helps you balance the true you, keeping old myths and messages tampered. Yes, they will creep back in, but with practice and daily commitment to being good and true to you, they will arise less and less often. When it becomes natural to live freely in your own identity, your Ego States chart will look like this.

CHAPTER 1

Tools in My Garage—How to Find Hope

I have a myriad of tools in my garage. I have every tool a person could ever want or need. I have new (complicated) power tools, old (rusty) tools, small tools, large tools, saws, and a box full of nails and screws of every size. I don't know how to use most of these tools, but I know they will come in handy once they end up at my mountain cabin.

This humble cabin, which I stumbled upon years ago in the mountains of North Carolina, is my haven, and it's in need of repair. Though I'm intimidated by doing the repairs myself, I know I have the tools to do so; I just have to learn how to use them. I have to step out of my comfort zone, ask someone to walk me through the best way to use the tools, and maybe even have that person help me get started. It's always uncomfortable asking someone for help. I'm very independent, but I also realize I can't be an expert at everything. I feel no shame in leaning on somebody with more experience to show me the ropes. Then I can pull out my own creativity and skills to get the job done. I am hopeful that once I start rejuvenating my little haven, the tools will feel natural in my hands, projects will flow one into the other, and the cabin will be renewed—as will I—by the success of my endeavors. I am prepared for some challenges along the way, but I trust that I will work through and learn from each one and keep looking forward to the next project.

If you're feeling hopeless and that your haven is in need of repair, my job is to teach you to use the tools you already possess (and maybe gain a few new ones) and to lend you my hope until you can find your own—until you are renewed and feel the success of your endeavors. With this book, you will rediscover the skills you've set aside, find joy in each day and in your natural abilities to problem solve, and be hopeful. Walls of insecurity will come down, and you'll realize you are strong and in control of your destiny.

We use numerous talents—no matter how tiny—to fill our days with positive results, yet sometimes we fall into a well of hopelessness for one reason or another and get lost in the turmoil of life. When we lose hope, we tend to focus on what's not right rather than on what is.

In the blank space below, list what is true, right, and just in your life, and what brings you joy.

Do you have skills that earn top accolades at work, or talent in the kitchen that puts Martha Stewart to shame? Maybe you lift others up when they are in need of encouragement, or find time to lend a hand to those in need.

Make a list of things that you already know how to do.

What motivates you to get out of bed every day and excel at the items above? Enjoyment? Self-satisfaction? Feeling in control?

You've listed your strengths and what motivates you. Now think about what you would like to learn more about. There must be something you've always wanted to try but have been afraid to, or maybe you don't want to devote the time. Let's say you've always wanted to learn a new language, but you think you can't because you were never good at those classes in school. Or maybe you're mathematically inclined and great at itemizing and calculating numbers, but language was never your strong suit. Chances are you'll be good at organized studying and can use your math skills to make sense of the new language in a unique way.

Take the ways in which you thrive and transfer those abilities to learning the new endeavor, and you'll be spreading your skills like mayonnaise.

Write down a couple of new skills you'd like to learn—no matter how frivolous they seem.

You may be thinking, *What does all of this have to do with hope? I'm struggling with chronic illness, and I'm about to lose my job.* As I lend you my hope, you will be reinforcing your inner strength and will keep focusing on the things in your life that keep you going. Each morning, you may have to overcome the voice in your head that says you don't have it in you to work all day, yet you do it no matter how bad you feel. Is it income that motivates you? What if you lost that income? You'd somehow find the energy to get another job because of your determination to have a roof over your head. As I teach you how to use the shovel you already own—that which gives you the courage to dig deep and find the fortitude to fight your struggles and keep looking ahead—you will discover a shred of hope one day, and then maybe a little more another day and so on.

Merriam-Webster's definition of *hope* is "to cherish a desire with expectation; to desire with expectation of obtainment; or to expect with confidence." Hope is a verb; it is an action, an expectation that there will be a result to an action taken. If you hope for a better life, take action to create the outcome of that hope. Hope is based on action and faith—knowing that things will get better and actually doing something to make them better.

Now take *optimism*. *Merriam-Webster* defines it as "a feeling or belief that good things will happen in the future; a feeling or belief that what you hope for will happen." It is a thinking process, a wish. Notice that *hope* is in the definition. Being optimistic is feeling hopeful that a certain event will take place once an action has moved you toward an outcome.

Many years ago, my daughter Kristin died at nearly two years of age due to a doctor's negligence. Through the immense grief, anger, desperation, and many other feelings one experiences in loss, hope never left. Optimism was gone, missing from my days, but hope never left. In fact, after living through Kristin's death, hope was stronger than ever. I had hope for happier days, hope that my experience could help others, and hope that the reason for her death would be clear to me eventually. I possessed the strongest hope that no matter what lay ahead for the rest of my days, I would get through it with strength and love.

When we are repeatedly beaten down by life, it is very hard to see our way clear of the frustration, the anger, the apathy, and the hurt. We lose self-confidence and feel sad, defeated, and lost. Throughout your journey, you are going to learn to let go of feelings that render you hopeless, and you will find your self-confidence by using the tools you already have while also gathering a few new ones. And little by little, hope will return, and there will be joy again, despite life's challenges.

I look forward to helping you learn how to use your tools, refresh your skills, and start to move forward through life in a healthy, uplifting way. This book is not going to tear you down or criticize or judge. You do that to yourself enough already. My hope is for you to understand that you are human, and neither your mistakes nor your childhood define you. Like any skill, finding snippets of joy takes practice. It's a daily exercise that starts with lifting yourself up, finding your strength, and knowing that no matter what befalls you, you can still find peace and love regardless of what society, your past, or your insecurities tell you.

Maybe you've heard some of this before, but this book is different. It will supply you with useful, personalized tools to use as you walk through life. But for this moment, let me lend you my hope.

> "Once we believe in ourselves we can risk curiosity, wonder, spontaneous delight or any experience that reveals the human spirit."
> — E.E. Cummings

Spiritual Hierarchy of Needs

Start therapy moving from one to the next,
focusing on Hope.

Ultimately, we want to live life equally between
Purpose and Hope.

CHAPTER 2

Choose Your Own Tune— How Did Childhood Messages Mold You?

There he is, whistling again, I thought frequently throughout my childhood, and it made me smile. I'm pretty sure it was Dad's way of making it through each day cheerfully. My mother, Catherine, was beautiful, thin, and a proper lady. We were poor as dirt, but that never stopped her from looking lovely when she ventured out. Sadly, whistling didn't stop alcoholism from claiming Dad, and beauty didn't make Mother a positive person—toward herself or others.

They were getting by in life with two children when—surprise!—I showed up. I'm told I was born happy. I guess that means I didn't cry a lot and was easy to handle (though that didn't last). Like all children, I thought my parents were the smartest people in the world, until I was old enough to read their verbal and nonverbal messages. Some of their messages were damaging, while others still inspire laughter today. "If you don't wear deodorant, you won't have any friends." I overheard this tidbit from my mother when I was in elementary school. She continued, "It's a Sure thing…a Right Guard…a Secret." *This one's a keeper,* I told myself then, and I still laugh when I remember that day, thinking, *true that!*

My dad, Cecil (otherwise known as Mr. Magoo because of his glasses), was a carpenter with perfect aim for the nail head—well, almost perfect. Even with his skills, he busted his thumb several times over forty years in the business. I can still hear him telling me, "If you're going to hit the nail, hit the damn thing!" He never wanted me to do anything half-assed. I haven't strayed from this advice, and it has been very successful for me.

Messages we receive as children can take us wherever we choose, and I will admit that many of the messages I received left me not knowing where to turn or what to do. One of those messages was that if you drank alcohol, you were an alcoholic, so I chose not to ever drink. I was in my thirties and had worked in ministry for years before I realized the myth in that statement, though I've continued to abstain due to my addictive personality.

I grew up behind an IGA grocery store and a laundromat. We were one paycheck away from the housing projects, and I knew I wanted more. I was determined not to stay there, not to struggle daily like my family did. Growing up this way strengthened me; the lessons were most valuable. Being poor didn't dash my lust for living, and existing in a house of alcoholism and destructive attitudes created the rock on which I still stand—lessons learned.

Mother dun told me, "Go to church, read your Bible, and do the right thing, and good things will happen to you." As my life streamed by, again I realized there wasn't a shred of truth in that simplistic advice. People have a way of saying things that can drastically alter our lives positively and negatively. Mothers and fathers have a way of making us scratch our heads and wonder if we'll make it in this big, scary world. Many of the messages and myths that we assume or are taught may take years to face and dispel. I've cried, survived, and even thrived despite those tough lessons, and you can too.

Mother dun told me. Daddy dun said. **How did messages from your parents mold you? Did they make you strong, fragile,**

sensitive, or angry? (Make a list below. We will get back to it in a minute).

What was the message?   How did it mold you?
For example:

Be perfect.   *I feel like a failure whenever I make a mistake.*

Shortly before my mother died, I overheard a friend of hers ask, "Who selected Cecilia's name, you or her dad?" Mother replied, "Her name could've been Buster Brown for all I cared." Ouch! As a child I had picked up on her uncaring feelings and believed she regretted naming me Cecilia after my dad, Cecil. No Boo-Boo Bunny could take that sting away, and God knows we all have lots of ouches from our childhood. Some of them hurt as much as a ball hitting us upside the head. We cry, shake off the hurt, stand tall, and try again, all through life. Know that it is okay to cry. There's nothing to be ashamed of, and as adults, we can *choose* the outcome of how those messages affect us. "Keep your eye on the ball and swing again," a coach would say. Whether we decide to swing or not is our decision.

We have all danced to the *Mother dun told me, Daddy dun said* tune. When you hear those voices in your head (and trust me, you do), stop listening and choose *your* truths; explore which ones are not working in your life. Decide today which voices and tunes you will *choose* to listen to, and delete the ones that stymie your laughter and spirit.

Take the messages from your list above and cross off the ones you don't want to listen to anymore—those that have stunted your personal growth. Highlight those that have served you well. Add more

9

positive actions and thoughts that you know you're capable of but make you feel vulnerable. For example, maybe trusting others makes you feel naked because you've been burned, but you know trusting people is a positive way to embrace life. Getting burned does happen, but turn it around and ask yourself how many times you will benefit by trusting others.

Now that you've started reading this book and have completed the first couple of exercises, are you committed to going forward and healing your burdened soul by dispelling old messages that steal your ability to find happiness and serenity? Together we are going to change your mixed messages, teach you to trust yourself and others, and discover how to be your best self by taking daily baby steps.

You're going to do some hard work that will challenge what you know to be true and open your world to a more relaxed, accepting, and joyful life. I highly recommend that you complete the exercises in each section in order to gain the most benefit. These short exercises are the same ones I give to clients to work on at home after they leave my office, and then we discuss their findings at their next appointment. It is an amazing transformation when one of the assignments clicks and the person's whole demeanor changes. It is usually the beginning of life-affirming change. In the end, this book will be your workbook, a tool whenever life gets you down or you start to slip into old habits.

Today is your time—right now—to throw off mixed messages, listen to your own music of life, and play your best game to live the life you want.

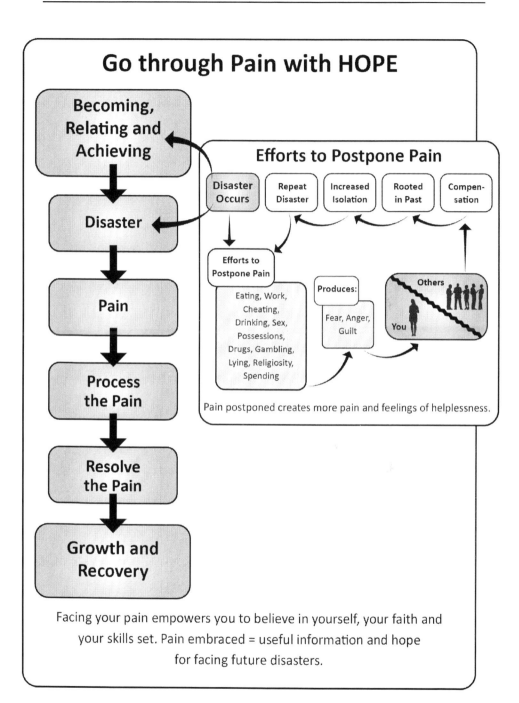

CHAPTER 3

Lessons from My Older Sister—Stop Judging, Start Trusting

My sister contracted HIV from a postsurgical blood transfusion in a Texas hospital. Two years and three months later, on August 31, 1989, she died. That day changed the course of my life permanently.

By age, she was my older sister, but her actions spoke otherwise. She was funny and mischievous, adventurous and outspoken, yet she was also naïve. She could pull off going on a date with one boy, coming home in the nick of time, showering, and then going out with another boy on the same night. When I was a child, she included me in everything and put up with my bed-wetting incidents. During sleepovers with her best friend, she would put two beds close together and make me sleep in the middle so I wouldn't pee on them. Since I always tagged along to flag corps practice, the team crowned me Honorary Mascot. My sister was my role model. She made me laugh, and her vibrancy made me want to be like her.

When I ponder our childhood, I reflect on the fact that we grew up in the same household, and though Dad didn't treat her well, she was always positive. I watched my sister learn survival tactics from Mother to deflect the minor damage from Dad's words. My mother and sister both turned a blind eye to the alcoholism and the verbal abuse.

My sister married at age nineteen. Though I was only twelve, I recognized that she was settling to get out of our house. Always outspoken, I let her know every chance I got that I hated what she was doing. I lashed out when she chose a male relative of her fiancé instead of me to sing at her wedding. I was jealous—she knew I was a powerful singer; my voice was one to be reckoned with. I couldn't believe that she chose him to sing over me, her own sister. I decided she needed my opinion, and after forcefully telling her how horrible I thought he sounded, her hand flew up with the speed of lightning and *whap*! My face felt like it was across the room. I was stunned. She had never hit me before, and I quickly realized I probably shouldn't have been so outspoken.

As time moved on, we had many loud disagreements about her life. I was very verbal in my opinions about how she was living, and I'm sure there were times when she wanted to slap me again, though she never did. One night when I was sixteen, I was having dinner at her house when I realized just how abusive her husband was. We were eating spaghetti, and in the blink of an eye, he smashed a plate of spaghetti all over the wall. Her children's eyes were as big as pancakes as he told us to clean up the mess. Being one who didn't take abuse from anyone, I stood up and reminded him, "I didn't make this mess, and I'm not cleaning it up. You do it!" He glared at me with a death stare as if to say, "How dare you!" I took the kids for a walk and returned when I felt it was safe. I noticed the mess had been cleaned up, and not another word was said.

As I entered my twenties, the rules of my sister's world continued to tighten. My brother-in-law wouldn't allow me to wear shorts or slacks in their house, only dresses, so I stopped going. I was always on my soapbox about injustice (the way *I* defined injustice, that is) and judging others, including my sister, for putting up with those injustices. Then one day, many years later, my sister made me aware of my own prejudices by pointing out how much she struggled. With resignation and apathy, she delcared, "I have six-monthed my way through this marriage for twenty-five years. I can do this for six more months...I can do this for six more months...just six more months."

I was shocked. As I picked up the pieces of my broken heart, I realized the jaded messages she had received growing up: "You made the commitment, so stick to it. You made your bed, now lie in it. Never give up....Always try harder and harder...one more time." And on it went.

When my sister contracted HIV from a blood transfusion, I was in my midthirties. HIV soon turned to AIDS, and once again, I expressed my anger. I told her how I despised the people who had given her that dreaded, horrific disease. "You don't deserve it," I said to her. I'll never forget her grabbing me by the nape of my neck, pulling me to her face, and scolding me as only a sister can do. "Don't ever talk like that again. No one *deserves* this disease. Look around at my funeral. All of my gay friends and those who have helped me through this will be there—some of them fighting this disease too. Do they deserve it? No! You're wrong. Grow up."

Those are some of the wisest words anyone has ever said to me. Amid her dealing with physical and emotional agony, and reflecting on how she had settled for an abusive marriage she never wanted, she confronted my cynicism and made me aware of my own judgement once again. "Grow up, sister. No one deserves to live with things that plague him or her forever. Stop judging."

I'm aware now of the people along the way who tried to kick my butt and get me to open my eyes to my jaded opinions, yet it took tragedy for me to see the value of stepping out of myself and considering others' life stories, including their misfortunes and struggles. It took my very own heartbreak to look beyond my blind spots and stop judging, and I'm a therapist, for goodness' sake.

Many of us grow up being told verbally and nonverbally what to do and what not to do until we eventually lash out with a vengeance, fed up with not knowing how to be in the world, with not being true to our natural personalities. In my case, when I feel threatened or see injustice, I want to fight with hurtful words. I have to take a step back, consider the situation, be aware of my prejudices, and keep my spiteful words out of it.

We all have blind spots. We look at others and judge their lives as we knowingly hide our own faults and our own secrets. We gloss over our deepest insecurities and pain and truly believe that nobody knows what we're hiding or coping with. Well, they know, because it's written all over us. It's in the way we act, the things we say, and the judgments we pass about others as we hide our deep feelings of guilt, loneliness, fear, inadequacy, rage, helplessness, or hopelessness.

Other times, the things that plague us are secrets even to ourselves—those are the issues that are painful to crack open, to admit. We've all had people we know well, or even a stranger, help us with a revelation that opens a door to our secrets and forces us to face our jaded selves. We then have an opportunity to grow and evolve, or we can turn away and close the door because it's too uncomfortable.

The Johari Window

Developed by Joseph Luft and Harry Ingham to show mainly two ideas:

- We can build trust between each other by sharing of ourselves
- We can learn about ourselves and come to terms with personal issues by acknowledging and acting on the feedback and help from others

Take time now to write a list of the people in your life who have opened those doors to make you look deeper at your own insecurities—those issues you know you need to address but turn away from. Who is it that pushes and prods you to move outside of your comfort zone to face what holds you back? Why do those particular individuals challenge you? Is it because they love you and want a better life for you? Trust them and let them guide you.

Make a list of your jaded ideas and prejudices, and write down how you think they're holding you back. Next to each idea, jot down one word that can open your eyes to the freedom from negative thoughts and actions. Do you feel free? Does it feel like you've let out a big sigh and a burden has been lifted?

Jaded Ideas and Prejudices	How is this holding me back?	Freeing Word
For example: *Overweight people are weak.*	*A work friend is overweight, and I think less of her because of that.*	*Acceptance*

I discourage you from six-monthing your way through life and settling because of your own prejudices. If you sit in judgment of others, your life will be dark and lonely, and you'll make choices out of regret and insecurity. Turn on the light, open the doors, sit quietly, and listen. What do you hear? What do you see for your life's possibilities? You choose—jaded myths, or the freedom to be open to others' truths, including your own.

"Actions do speak louder than words so pay attention to how you behave before correcting someone else's behavior."

— **Cecilia Tucker**

CHAPTER 4

Pull Up Your Big-Kid Panties—First Steps to Empowering Yourself

Finally, first grade! I thought, excited and eager to learn. I noticed that Chucky, the little boy who sat next to me, had a shoe untied. I bent over to tie it and quickly scrambled back up to see what was happening on top of my head. My very young, vibrant teacher was thumping my head as if I were an animal. Thump! Thump! Thump! Three times to get my attention. She made me look into her eyes, which was scary to a little bitty person, pointed her finger, and scolded me. "Don't do that! If you keep doing things like that, he'll never learn to take care of himself. Let him learn to tie his own shoes."

My heart raced. I knew better than to speak. Instead, I promptly removed myself to the coatroom and shut the door. I stomped my little six-year-old feet as loudly as I could on the wooden floor and bellowed, "Someday I'll help whoever I want, and you won't be able to stop me!"

I realize now that, in that moment, I had found my voice and made a decision. I wasn't going to be silent and powerless. At the tender age of six, the message I received was that I had no power and no voice and that my actions were wrong. Even my very young teacher, whom I looked up to, was trying to mold me. She shut me down. It was then that I started taking a stand against the insidious things people said to me. I refused to be told what I could and couldn't do, who I could and couldn't be, and what I could and couldn't say. I wasn't going to pretend to feel the way others felt or believe what others believed just to save face.

We all have detrimental childhood stories that still mold our opinions and actions and go against how we really feel. These events alter our entire lives as we stuff our true feelings and become "yes" people. If we keep them in our "unawares" and they become part of us, even though deep inside we know they're not our truths, we stay immature and live in a pretend world.

We keep wearing the shoes and clothes (i.e., the myths and messages) of a child. They keep us from being the grown-up, empowered people we were created to be. As an adult, what child-sized clothes and shoes are you still trying to squeeze into? This might include pretending and lying in order to be liked. (Make a note if you need to.) Those clothes must be uncomfortable, yet you keep wearing them and don't speak up for yourself. How many times have you discovered yourself trying to be someone you're not and feeling powerless to step forward and be the person you truly want to be?

In chapter 2, we identified some myths and messages and how they molded you. In greater detail below, list all of the things people have told you that you *should, ought, must, never,* and *always do or not do.*

Should, Ought, Must, Never, Always	Adult Decision	Adult Action
For example:		
Never take risks.	*Apply for dream job.*	*Leave old, steady job for new venture.*

Write each childhood message, action, and adult decision on a three-by-five-inch index card or individually on the pages of a small note-pad. Take the stack of *should/ought/must/never/always* and rip up each card, then toss the pieces into the trash — this will add to your satisfaction of letting go. Now take the adult-decision sections and reexamine them. Are these helping you express the real you? Are you getting the results in life that you desire? If not, send them to the trash with the others.

Now look at the remaining cards and make sure these will lead you to behaviors that will help you be your best self. Keep them with you and refer to them whenever you hear the *shoulds* or the *nevers* creeping in, or if your self-esteem nose-dives due to another's judgment. Practice being your *true* self every day, and it will become second nature. What a big step you just accomplished!

> *"Lessons learned are often caught not taught."*
>
> **— Cecilia Tucker**

CHAPTER 5

Pilot Rock—Don't Be Afraid of What You Want from Life

I was sixteen, and what I was about to do would be a life-changing experience. Every Sunday, Dad dropped me off at church. I enjoyed attending, though he never did and Mother did so rarely. At this particular service, I stood at the back of our Baptist church, holding on for dear life to the pew in front of me, anxiously waiting for my opportunity. I looked around, glancing from one parishioner to the next. I thought of Mother's disapproval and Dad's encouragement and felt my nerves rattle as I held tightly to the belief that I was going to be who I wanted to be.

The invitation was given to accept Christ as Savior and Lord, and to recommit to Jesus after straying from God's will (all you Southern Baptists know what that's about), then the congregation bellowed the fifteenth verse of "Just as I Am." I slowly let go of the pew, and on shaky legs, I made my way down the aisle. I stood before our intelligent, articulate pastor, a man I had great respect for, and proudly announced, "God has called me into ministry." I will never forget the next breath, the moment when he paused, looked right through me, and said, "Cecilia, God doesn't call women to ministry. God calls them to be preachers' wives or maybe teachers and nurses in the missionary field, but not preachers."

He drove a stake through my heart. You see, I grew up in that church. I trusted my pastor. All my life I had been told that God loved all people. I'd been encouraged by the church to find my voice, to sing, and to stand up in front of a congregation of a thousand week after week to share how God shined his grace upon me. Yet when I felt called by God, which was what I thought it meant when God touched you, I was shut down. The book was slammed shut on me like someone slamming a book on a table. The thud was so loud it pierced my heart. I felt stuck.

Following my silence, which felt like hours, he said, "You must be mistaken, for God doesn't call women to ministry."

The awkward voice of a sixteen-year-old girl—my voice—said to this powerful man, "In my eyes, somebody *is* mistaken, but I don't think it's God or me."

As I stood in front of the trusted pastor who had just betrayed me, a revelation hit me in that life-affirming moment: I needed something to pilot me—a new, untainted view of God. I needed to cast off the old, traditional church views that had been drilled into me from a very young age and find an unbiased (and proverbial) rock to lean on—my own rock.

Well, it turned out I found a real rock—Pilot Rock. Every Sunday afternoon from that moment on, after regular church services, I found myself with friends at a place near the water, and *in* the water I would stand. There was a rock in the middle of a small lake that became my pulpit, and the preaching began to my friends standing on the nearby shore. I repreached what I'd learned that morning at church and add a twist of humor, laughing and inspiring others' laughter. My sermons were about David and Bathsheba, the four spiritual laws, and the Roman road to salvation. I'd expound on the hymn "Just as I Am without One Plea" and sermonize about giving everything to God. I knew there were profound and humorous messages in those sermons that were true for all of God's creation, not just for men.

The pastor's hurtful words created a triumphant woman who became ordained at twenty-nine years of age, and thirty-four years later,

I'm still a minister. Pilot Rock started my journey into the ministry, and that journey led me to preach within several denominations over many years.

Just a few years ago, I was ousted from my church for standing my ground on a political matter, for being true to myself once again. Now, most Sundays I find myself not on a rock, but preaching at a waterside park, much like when I started. And when I go to my humble cabin up north, I preach on the mountain in someone's home. The vestibule may change, but the calling remains the same. I still stand up for who I want to be; I say *yes* to my instincts and own my truths.

Now it's your time to decide where your Pilot Rock will be. Where will you take a stand to be your true self?

In the previous sections, you identified the jaded messages you received from a parent or loved one about your value as a person, who you're supposed to be and how you're supposed to act, and how all of it molded your beliefs and actions. You made a plan to discard those mixed messages and begin to admit your truths. By now I hope you realize you no longer have to trust that the restrictions set upon you as a child—and those set daily in your adult life—are the truth. But I suspect there's still something holding you back: societal pressure.

Let's identify which myths institutions and society put upon you. **What have you grown up believing about yourself that doesn't reflect the real you?** Some beliefs may overlap with your previous list, but that will make it easier to identify which ones have really shaped you, and you can prioritize eliminating those from your life.

What institutions have shut you down and discouraged you from being who you truly want to be?

What groups have you tried to associate with, only to be told or have it be insinuated that you're not gifted enough, or that you're not the right gender, the right race, the right size, or the right sexual orientation?

Say aloud, "Yes, I can be a member of _____. Yes, I can _____. Yes, I do have these gifts and talents: _____. Yes, this is my calling. This is who I am. Yes, I count." Eliminate the negative. Nothing is impossible. Be courageous, and in the next week or two, act on at least one *yes*. Stand on your Pilot Rock and do something you were told you couldn't do.

CHAPTER 6

YTF—Start by Redefining Your Reflection

The sorority is called "You're Too Fat" (YTF). When I grew up, size mattered—just as it does now. Somehow, supersizing our food is acceptable, but supersizing our bodies is not. When I was younger and I saw clothing labeled size 0 or size 2, I thought the tags were missing a number. I'd turn the tag over or look inside the shirt, thinking that I must have missed something. *This must be 04 or 06.... Maybe the 2 should be 12.* I'll admit I was baffled.

Skip ahead. I'm touring a university campus with my daughter. We're being shown around by this cute little twenty-something assistant, and she notices one of the other mothers has a keychain with Greek letters on it. The assistant asks about the sorority she was in, and the mother lights up with pride and tells her. Then she starts asking each mother what sorority they belonged to, and they proudly announce their affiliations. When she gets around to me, I say just as proudly, "I was in the YTF sorority." For about thirty seconds, she looks like she ate a lemon, and I figure she's probably reciting the Greek alphabet in her head. Finally she says, "I don't remember that one." In my not-so-diplomatic way, I replied, "Well, it *must* be Greek to you, but it's never been Greek to me. YTF is the You're Too Fat sorority."

Silence. I didn't mean to embarrass her; I was trying to be funny. Did I mean to make a point? Absolutely. You see, all of my life—*all of my life*—size has mattered. Just like being too short or too tall, having a funny nose or a big butt or the wrong-size boobs, or being the wrong gender matters. How many times have we heard or repeated, "It's not what's on the outside that defines us; it's who we are on the inside"? We say it and say it and say it. But it does not change the fact that we are judged on first impressions, and our outer shell matters in society.

> "Sticks and stones may break my bones but harsh words crush my spirit."
>
> — Cecilia Tucker

Most of us go through life stuck with a label and define ourselves by our imperfections. We forget to look at the gifts we have and completely ignore our intelligence, our kind spirit, or our sense of humor. We forget that maybe we have gorgeous eyes around that imperfect nose, or that our smile lights up a room despite the size of our hips. It is by far one of the hardest habits to break—to stop defining ourselves by what others think of us. Our bodies are only containers for our spirits, for our souls. I'll admit, even I get lost in worrying about the vessel and not caring for the spirit.

The You're Too Fat sorority can be any sorority—you're too stupid, smart, blond, brunette, gifted, clumsy, broken, depressed, miserable, happy, crazy, and so on. Every person has a *You're Too* _____.

What sorority (or fraternity) do you find yourself in? When you feel ready—maybe it will take thought, or maybe it's an immediate response—name it, stare it in the face, and practice a new mantra.

Take the *You're Too*_____ and rename it. Change it to your good attribute(s): *I am loyal, friendly, genuine, loving, kind,* or *compassionate.* Change your thinking and make a new decision every time you start to think about the so-called fault. *Stop* and think about your new definition.

27

When you look in the mirror and start the autotune of "I'm too fat/pale/short," *stop* and say, "I'm feeling healthy today, and I'm ready for _____." You will be amazed how your brain automatically peps up and you feel refreshed. You may even feel a smile creep up from your heart.

I'm too...	I *am*...	New Mantra
For example:		
Big	Healthy	I am ready to be strong and confident.

Open your mind, your vista, and your world. If you have a photo of yourself making eye contact with a parent, a sibling, or a friend, see the kindness and the smile in your eyes. Set that photo where you can see it often, and embrace yourself with that kindness. Think about "YTG" as your new Greek sorority: You're Too Good! You're just fine! You're not "BDW" (Broke, Don't Work), *and never forget that you are loved*. Your new eyes, ears, legs, and arms can move you through your insecurities and beyond the impasse that society has created, because you know the *real* you. And as always, if you can laugh at yourself a little and not take yourself too seriously, you've already started the process.

CHAPTER 7

Check Your Price Tag— Nurturing Self-Esteem

When my daughter Kara was about eight years old, she was in a gymnastics competition that went wrong at every turn, and her team lost. As all the other little girls were walking off the mat crying, Kara decided to lighten the mood by telling a joke. Without really thinking about what she was doing, and with all the confidence in the world, she started telling a joke about a stuttering Bible salesperson to a group of coaches on the sidelines. Shocked, I sat there thinking, *Oh, she is not telling* that *joke. It's so politically incorrect!* All of a sudden, there was laughter from everyone, and in that moment, her self-esteem soared because she knew she was funny. Humor lifted her out of the disappointment and broke the tension. *What a gift she has*, I remember thinking with relief.

As we grow, our self-esteem slowly develops, ranging from high to low, back to high, back to low, and so on. Entering adulthood— and sometimes sooner—our version of self becomes skewed by how others see us (e.g., YTF) and what they think of us. As long as we do the "right" things like get good grades, win awards, and procure promotions, external affirmation for those achievements makes our self-esteem soar. When we're complimented about the way we look, or when we're looked down upon because we dress differently, we take note and stop living by our own standards, as mentioned in chapter 6. The self-sabotage is even bigger on a subconscious level. The insecurities that societal pressure starts creating in childhood can be deeply damaging.

Kara telling that joke and my reaction to her is a perfect example of one of the ways childhood self-esteem can be broken or created. I could have scolded her for telling an inappropriate joke, but instead I praised her for her ability to carry on and find humor in a difficult time. As parents, teachers, and caregivers, it is easy to bestow praise on kids when they get good grades or achieve accolades, and it's just as easy to scold them or make them say they're sorry for making an honest mistake or for being who they need to be in a particular moment. When children act out or speak out, it's usually their way of finding themselves and their voices. It may not be socially acceptable behavior, but if you can find something good in what they've said or done, let them know.

One of the best ways to build children's self-esteem is by praising them when they're not expecting it, like when they're thoughtful. For example, my four-year-old grandson has an amazing memory. He not only listens, but he also retains information that blows me away. When he repeats something detailed that he remembers from a previous conversation, I praise him by saying what a good listener he is and how wonderfully thoughtful he is. It is never too early to start helping children build their self-esteem, but there does come a time when it's too late. If they haven't gained self-respect and a consistent personality by the time they're young adults, they will tend to conform to outward ideals and become chameleons. By this time, if their confused self-image or lack of self-esteem has been cemented, they'll end up seeking love and acceptance in unhealthy ways throughout life.

Many of us go through life repeatedly changing our ideas of who we want to be and eventually end up full of self-doubt, which keeps us in a cycle of self-deprecation. When you look in the mirror, is your sense of self blurred between how you want to see yourself and how others see you? We all fear not belonging and at times devalue ourselves to fit in, to be part of a desired group. Everybody wants to belong, so it's easy to conform to what brings praise and not stay true to the little voice inside that nudges you to be *you*—hence the tug-of-war that brings discontent and low self-esteem. The self-esteem cycle is represented well in the movie *Runaway Bride*, especially when Richard Gere implies that Julia Roberts likes her eggs cooked whatever way her current boyfriend likes them.

If you lack self-esteem and have gone through life hiding behind a façade, you're probably unaware that it is insecurity and fear of not belonging that drives you. You may be stuck in a continual loop of wanting change rather than making change. If you don't like your life, you've probably tried to change the following:

1) Your environment (job, city, neighborhood, hangout)
2) The players (friends, associates, neighbors)
3) The game (being the victim, rescuer, or persecutor)
4) The other person's personality (whoever is blaming you or making you feel low)
5) Yourself (epiphany)

This pattern is how most individuals spend their lives as they try to change numbers one to four, one to four, one to four, until *bam!*—something changes that makes them finally look inside and ask, *Why do I keep repeating this exhausting regimen? What is it in me, or what am I lacking, to be consistently drawn into unhappy or complicated situations?* With the answers to that evaluation, they can finally arrive at number five, and the cycle will slow to a halt.

What has to change in your life for you to start freeing yourself from the chains of a perceived persona and the cycle above? The answer is *you*. If you start being truthful with yourself about who you are and what you want from life every single day, there will be fewer lies, the endless search for happiness will lessen, and there will be joy in each day. Without that self-truth, there can be no true love, no peace, no self.

The cliché "You can't love another until you first love yourself" is accurate. You cannot give your authentic self to another with fluctuating self-esteem. In order to love yourself, you will pull love from those around you until the well runs dry. If you're frequently dishonest, your self-esteem will sink lower and lower until you have a hard time looking others in the eyes, not to mention yourself. Be truthful, *use your words*, say what you mean, and do what you say you will.

Like most of us, I'm sure you look in the mirror daily and mutter something about your perceived shortcomings. Your hair is too thin or too curly, or you notice a new wrinkle and compare yourself to the perfect Hollywood ideal. If you ask yourself what your greatest qualities are, right away you'll name something you *do*, or you'll focus on a physical trait rather than defining who you are innately. Tough distinction.

Not sure if you can differentiate between "what I do" and "who I am"? In the previous chapter, you wrote a new mantra. **Write down five of those character traits listed under "I AM." Add a new one or two if it suits you—for example, honest, funny, kind, passionate, loving.**

Now ask five people you trust to do the same for you. It will feel odd asking, but tell them it's for a project, and they'll be happy to do it. **Write down the common traits they listed, including your own.**

Take this list, transfer it to a piece of paper, and then hang it on the mirror in your bathroom. You'll be referring to it morning and night as you wade through the clutter to discover the real you.

In order to find yourself, you'll have to be brave, dig deep, and admit who you are in your heart and what you want from *your* life—not what is expected of you. It's a big task, and it's not easy. In order to discover your true self, remember the following:

- Honesty comes first.
- Commit to taking the necessary steps to achieve the outcome you want for the right reasons.
- Set reasonable goals.

The most confident people I know stay faithful to their characteristics and set daily goals for personal growth. When you stick to your action plan and hold yourself accountable, you can look in the mirror at night and say, "I did it. I was honest today, and I stretched to learn something new." And from that comes instant self-esteem and satisfaction.

Commit to reading and *believing* the list on your mirror as you prepare for the day, saying to yourself, "I will be true to these attributes today." At night, as you get ready for bed, ask in return, "Was I the best I could be, and did I live up to these traits today?" If you're honest, you probably missed one or two. Don't fret and berate yourself; you're human. Vow to start anew the next day.

To begin setting goals for personal growth, start exploring how you envision the future *you* (maybe six months from now). Do you wish you were more patient or less prone to worry? **Write a list of characteristics that you would like to embrace or improve upon.**

Now make a timeline and work in reverse (see below). I call it backward planning. What goals would you like to achieve by the end of six months, and what steps can you take each day to get there? I'm not talking about work or external achievements. I'm talking about characteristics, a way to be in the world. For example, "In six months I would like to be more patient with others, healthier, more focused, and I would like to sing more." (Singing brings me joy.) Along the way, pay attention to your actions, be patient with yourself, and continue to set goals and work on them.

At the end of each day, assess your progress and be kind to yourself for the strides made, hold yourself accountable for the things you didn't do, and forgive the things you attempted but missed. For example, "Today I lost my patience at the grocery with the bagger and missed my boot camp class, though I'm proud to say I did sing. Tomorrow I will put the patience hat on again, and I will make it to my exercise class for a healthier me."

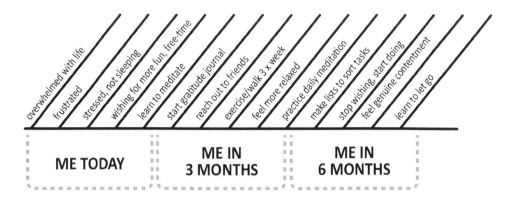

Example

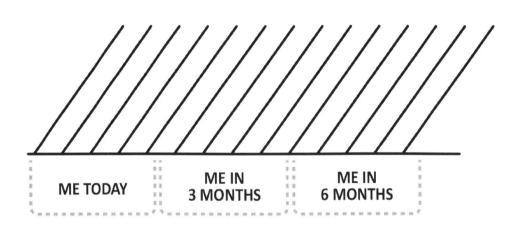

Day after day it will become easier, a way of life. And as you do this, your self-esteem will grow. You will look at your reflection and know who you are and where you are going, and you will start to like yourself again (or maybe for the first time).

After a few weeks of working on your timeline, you may notice a pattern of things that hold you back. You will have to ask yourself what circumstances repeat themselves and what commonality exists between them that continues to lower your self-esteem. I call it a "Me Blind Spot."

Once you discover your Me Blind Spot, go to those who have your best interests at heart and ask them to help you figure out why you keep repeating the same actions that garner the same results. For example, if you have a friend who continues to hurt your feelings, ask your trusted group what characteristic they see in you that allows your hurtful friend (an oxymoron, really) to lower your self-esteem. They may point out that you didn't feel loved as a kid, so you don't want to let anyone slip away; maybe you are afraid of being lonely. This will give you objective insight so that you can work on being strong and giving yourself permission to let your hurtful friend go. Be *true* to yourself.

This is a big chapter with many thought-provoking and even painful calls to action, because once you realize who you are, you will feel compelled to make some tough decisions, and with that comes change. But this time, change will be for the right reasons, and it will be permanent—a

> *"If you aren't being treated with love and respect, check your price tag. Maybe you've marked yourself down. It is you who tells people what your worth is. Get off the clearance rack and get behind the glass where they keep the valuables."*
>
> **— Author Unknown**

new way to be in the world. Once you get through the tough lessons, you will feel relief and self-respect for having the strength to stand tall. We get one chance at life, and spending it searching for fulfillment in false places leads to a hollow existence.

CHAPTER 8

Going to the Mountain—
Accepting Your Limitations

Not too many years ago, I was going to my little cabin in the mountains of North Carolina. My husband was supposed to be riding with me, but he wasn't able to take the time away from work, so I drove alone. Driving on Interstate 75 toward my hometown, as I had done hundreds of times, I found myself two and a half hours north of where I was supposed to have exited. When I figured out my error, I was furious. (That's putting it mildly.) I called my husband and told him it was his fault because if he had gone with me, I certainly wouldn't have gotten lost. I let him know *he* had to fix it.

He was stunned by my accusation and started laughing. You can imagine that I didn't find it funny. I was seething, and I was really lost. When he finally stopped laughing, my husband redirected me in the dark through the hills and backroads of Georgia until I was on the right road to my mountain, still two and a half hours away. I finally arrived safely, and after a sigh and a few minutes of downtime, I was able to laugh about it.

When I was seething, I had chosen to blame somebody else for my being lost instead of accepting that being directionally challenged is part of my humanness. It is a limitation that stops me in my tracks.

It limits my ability to visit new places and learn new things, and it ultimately limits my growth because I'm afraid I won't make it to my destination. And doesn't this self-imposed constraint leave me spiritually lost?

This trait will never go away, but I have to continue to push myself to drive to new places and realize that if I get lost, I will eventually find my way. Some of the most exciting things I've ever experienced have come from being directionally challenged. I discovered my cabin on the mountain, which is such a part of me now, by straying from the beaten path.

I'm in my sixties, and I continue to tell myself that being lost is not the end of the world. Instead I find it is a chance to ask, *What am I supposed to see here?* There are times when we learn the most from feeling really lost. Changing our attitude by turning it into a positive can make all the difference in overcoming our self-imposed constraints.

Accepting our limitations and redirecting our goals and attitude are a must. I'd like to tell you that as I've aged, my lack of navigational skills has improved, but it hasn't. I've had to learn how to live with it and within it and not let my fear of getting lost stop me from moving forward. I had to stop blaming and start taking responsibility for either fixing it or accepting it. When I realize that I'm not doing something out of fear of getting lost, I ask myself how many more times I will allow that fear to keep me from going places, emotionally and physically.

In previous chapters, you've examined the many messages, myths, truths, and labels that have helped shape your self-image. You've thrown some out, recognized a few that may be serving you well, and learned to look at yourself in a more positive light. While you continue daily exercises of nurturing your soul, remember that being human means you will have to overcome challenges, and learning how to accept the things you cannot change will strengthen your self-esteem.

Limitations are learned as children and young adults from our parents, caregivers, schoolteachers, and church leaders. Some limitations may also be due to genetic predispositions, self-abuse, or physical restrictions, yet the fear of stepping outside of those boundaries has shaped your life.

The first step in overcoming this fear is identifying your biggest limitation. What is it?

Who taught this limitation to you, or were you born with it?

Do you believe you are permanently limited, or can you change it?

How do you think others see you?

Are they wrong?

Right now, make a decision about whom you are going to believe. Are you going to continue to believe the restrictive message that stops you from living a free life, or are you going to recognize the positive outside validation from others who don't restrict you? When someone pays you a compliment, do you wave it off and say, "Oh, no, not me. You're so much better than I am"? Learn to say thank you, and feel proud of your accomplishments.

Whether your limitations were impressed upon you or they are genetic or physical, ask yourself if your imperfections make you a lesser person. Stop and think—are they real and true, or do you use them as an excuse to avoid being your best self? Do you have wishes and dreams in your head and utter "if only…" as you go through each day? You're probably playing the self-blame game because you know you're not living life to its fullest potential.

Chances are the choices you've made and the place you find yourself have led you to read this book and want to make changes. Changing yourself is one of the most difficult endeavors to take on and requires daily work. Here's a simple way to get started every morning when you wake up:

- Set your mind to being good to yourself and others.
- Make a checklist of things to do to stay healthy.
- Keep track of your accomplishments.

How am I good to myself and others?

My checklist of healthy choices:

List your accomplishments.

Keep doing this every day, even if it seems redundant. Your brain chemistry will start to change, but only with repetition. Refer back to the lists above for confirmation, and continue to turn to those you trust. At the end of the day, ask if you were good to yourself. Did you let your limitations control you, or was it your attitude? Let go of yesterday's imperfections, and look forward to new successes tomorrow.

Some adult limitations, let's use alcoholism for example, are the result of self-loathing (or escapism) that started at an early age. If you self-abuse (smoking, food, drugs), it has kept you from living a full life and will eventually present with physical ailments that will keep you down. Every day that passes, you make excuses for why you can't stop now. Self-abuse can only be overcome with emotional work, recognizing what led to the abuse in the first place, admitting it is a crutch and sincerely wanting to move forward.

Examples of limitations that may provide an excuse to not live your life to the fullest; never realizing it is up to you to find a way around them.

- **Physical Limitations:** Loss of limb, sight, hearing, Degenerative Disease, RA, Scoliosis, etc.

- **Genetic Limitations:** High or low IQ, Autism, Diabetes, Heart Disease, Too Tall or Short, Thyroid Disease, Celiac, etc.

- **Mental:** Depression, Bi-Polar, Childhood Mental or Physical Abuse, IQ, Social Anxiety, Mental Disorders

CHAPTER 9

Basket Toss in the Dark— Letting Go of Fear and Worry

W here is she? I thought breathlessly. Is she safe? Who has her? I was sitting in a huge gymnasium watching my twelve-year-old daughter cheerlead. She was new to competitive cheerleading, and to be honest, I had always thought it was a wussy, girlie sport. But this particular day, sitting among hundreds of other cheerleader parents, I proudly watched my daughter being thrown up in the air. As she reached the pinnacle of a basket toss, the lights went out. Complete darkness. No emergency lights came on. I was blind. My heart raced as I worried what the outcome of the toss would be.

Finally, moments later, after fear had held me in its grip, and I had no idea what had happened to Kara, the lights came on and I saw her standing out on the floor. My daughter had been caught safely! Those few moments of panic in the darkness had scared me, and I realized it was comparable to trusting and stepping out in faith. I had to see my way through the darkness, and when the lights came on, all was fine.

In the struggles of life, when all the lights go out and we feel to-tally out of control, we know we have to step forward, but so many of us don't. We are paralyzed with fear and worry. Does this sound familiar? Do you struggle with fear and lack trust in your decisions because it's easier to stay in the dark? Do you project *what-ifs* with every situation until you make no decision at all? If you are nodding your head, now is the time to step forward in the dark—into the un-known—and trust that when the lights are out, you'll be caught. What other option is there?

If you spend all of your time standing idle in the dark, holding your breath with your hands full of what you already know, you can't move forward with growth or faith in the unfamiliar. Do a little experiment with me right now. Make a fist with both hands. Now with clasped hands, pick up a pencil in each hand. You can't do it. You're hands are full—full of whatever you are holding on to. Nothing new can enter or be gained. And I bet you were holding your breath as you tried to pick up that pencil.

I always laugh at the line in the movie *City Slickers*: "I sell air. All I sell is air." I'm amazed at how much air we hold, as we hold our own breath, hoping to avoid places where the light is absent. It ends up being stale air full of worry and anxiety. Hear me when I say this: you cannot step forward until you find the courage to walk into the dark, through your fear of the unknown, and to allow a trusted friend or loved one to catch you if you fall.

The art of being a good flyer in competitive cheerleading is trusting that the people around you will catch you. Does it always happen that way? No, it does not. Bad things do happen to cheerleaders who are flyers. Scary things can happen to those of us who take a chance and jump, fly, step, or crawl into a new circumstance. Life is full of choices, full of opportunities, and if you stay on the ground in the dark in your sure and true-and-tried way of life, you will not experience what's just beyond your closed fist to help you learn, grow, and expand.

Think about the different times in your life when you've had the opportunity to jump but said, "No, thank you." How about all the times you chose the safe road and said, "Not me; I don't think I want to take the chance—not again. I've been down that road and don't like where it led"? How about, "You go; I'll watch. You don't know my past, so I'm not going to trust that it's the right road for me just because you said so"? Have there been times when you've uttered, "When I get more facts, maybe then I'll take the step. Huh? Trust you? I don't think so"?

If you finish your story with one of these excuses and limit yourself with the lights dimmed, you'll never grow, you'll never find release, and you may go out of this world muttering to yourself, "Shoulda, coulda, woulda."

So how do you move into the light, stop worrying, and start trusting the unknown? Start by closing your hands again and holding your breath. Clasp so tightly that you dig nails into your flesh, just for a second or two. Now open your hands and let out your breath. Can you feel the freedom and easing of anxiety throughout your mind and body? Try it again.

Now open your arms and shake them while sticking your chest out and take deep, cleansing breaths. Does this help you feel open to something new? When you open your physical body, your brain automatically feels uplifted. You take in more joy, more love, and more life. It seems too simple, I know. But if you practice, it starts to happen naturally, without needing the physical clenching and opening.

When you start to have a doubtful moment, and a fear of trusting or trying something new arises—for example, if you have a major life decision staring you in the face, and you really want to leap at the chance but you're afraid—then try the exercise above. It may feel a bit silly, but it's a strong metaphor for what you've been doing emotionally to stay in the dark. Do this simple exercise enough and uncertainty will lift, and you'll see more clearly which way to go.

> "Worrying erases the present, adds nothing to tomorrow and can't change the past. Worrying is wasted energy that lacks positive results."
>
> — *K. Sadler*

It may be uncomfortable to be brave and stop worrying, but the reward is there, on the edge of darkness where it starts to brighten. You'll feel invigorated and proud of overcoming your fear of the dark and will gain confidence. Now you're living in the light.

CHAPTER 10

Flat on My Face!—Laugh and Accept That You Are Human

have been a minister for forty-three years, and I have performed weddings, funerals, and sermons. I have spoken at public venues, led seminars and workshops, and not once have I fallen. Tripped, oh, yes—I've tripped a few times. Pretty light on my feet, I have always been able to recover, except for one particular occasion. I fell hard. Flat. On. My. Face. The story goes like this.

My son's wedding was about to begin. All the t's had been crossed, the i's dotted, and everything had gone as planned. I was feeling proud that we had beautifully orchestrated the wedding. People had arrived on time; there were no stragglers, nobody lost, and no hurriedness, even in the final moments before the walk down the aisle. I was elated to be performing the ceremony and had spent hours upon hours preparing for this perfect day. My part went smoothly, and as I finished, I looked proudly at my son and his new wife, knowing that all was well with them. This was a great day, a life-changing day. I had married hundreds of other couples before, but this was very different. My only son, my child, was now a husband.

As the last person in the wedding party left the sanctuary, it was my turn to proceed into the vestibule. I was standing next to the associate pastor, and the signal came to start walking. As I stepped forward, trying to miss the other pastor's foot, I fell! I was in my robe, flat on my face in front of two hundred and fifty people. Everyone was staring, waiting for the last of us to head toward the receiving line, and I was literally on my face. A few people rushed to the scene to help. I popped up (with a little help from my nephew) like a jack-in-the-box and sprang to my feet, shaking it off like "I meant to do that!" I was stunned and embarrassed as I made my way out the back door and straight to the bathroom, where a faithful friend followed me in.

As my friend and I were putting Humpty-Dumpty back together in order to face all of the gatherers at the reception (and restore some dignity), I started laughing. What in the world was I going to do? I laughed and laughed and couldn't believe that after all I had done to make the day perfect, it had still gone wrong. I had still fallen flat on my face.

As I stood up from the bathroom vanity, an eye-popping fact sprang to mind. Eyes wide, I exclaimed to my friend, "Oh, no! I'm wearing Spanx today! Did I fall with my feet toward the congregation, or did I fall with my feet toward the altar?"

She thought for a moment as she tried to remember. Then she said with relief, "You fell with your feet toward the altar."

"Phew! Well, then, it was only God who got to view my Spanx and not the congregation. Thank you, God!" And we laughed even more.

I finally left the restroom, entered the reception, and participated in the celebration proudly. To my relief and surprise, nobody mentioned my not-so-graceful exit. I reminded myself what I had been teaching others over the years: when you fall flat on your face (literally or metaphorically), pick yourself up, find some humor, accept what has happened, and talk yourself into moving forward.

When you fall down, one of the most important things you can do is laugh. Don't take yourself too seriously. I've told my son and daughter-in-law that if they ever get in a pinch and need some money, they have my permission to send the video of my fall to *America's Funniest Home Videos*. All I ask is that I get a small share of the winnings.

It's your turn to reminisce. **Write down the times when you think you've fallen on your face and failed. How did you treat yourself? Did you berate yourself and let it cause fear? Next to each instance, reframe it with humor. How might you look at each time as funny?**

Times When I've Failed	How did I treat myself?	How was it actually funny?

This exercise will help you accept that you're human and not feel bad about yourself. Embrace who you are and remember that life is always going to offer up challenges—so laugh. Next time you label a faux pas as *bad* or *wrong*, try to find one bit of humor in it and give yourself a break.

> According to the University of Virginia and Mayo Clinic, "The average child laughs 300 to 500 times per day while the average adult laughs only 15 times per day. Laughing helps control stress by stimulating organs, relieving the stress response, soothing tension, improving immune function, relieving pain and increasing satisfaction" Not to mention what it does for your frown lines. So lighten up and allow MORE laughter into your days.

CHAPTER 11

Did Someone Die and Appoint You God?— Parenting 101

I had only been a parent for a couple of years, but already my son, Kevin, was finding issues with my parenting style. There were many times when my son was matter-of-fact about his beliefs and I would stifle a laugh, because he would be very adult-like and earnest, trying to clue me in to what he needed, but sadly, I missed the seriousness. At times I overlooked the truths in his statements or the type of encouragement he needed and found my parenting stuck in a loop where I stopped growing. Old behaviors recur even though we think we know better.

Subconsciously, I taught my children many of the subtle myths and messages I had soaked up as a child. The very same myths I swore I would not instill in my own children slipped into my parenting skills. It took years to realize I was perpetuating the same patterns, tripping over the same issues, or forcing the opposite to happen instead of letting awareness of my childhood history and instincts govern my choices. It took each of my children, in their matter-of-fact childhood honesty, to point out to me that what I was doing or saying didn't make sense or that I wasn't "getting it," and then I would realize my own issues were ruling the situation.

When Kevin was ten years old, we were having an argument. I had come home after a bad day and was short-tempered with him. I lost my patience over an unfinished chore and demanded that he "do it now," as parents often do. Instead of pouting or acting hurt, he looked up at me and demanded, with hands on his hips, "Did someone die and appoint you God, and I missed the ceremony?" Speechless for a moment and not knowing whether to stifle a laugh or be angry, I snapped back, "No, you didn't miss the ceremony!" I know some parents would've found this retort disrespectful, but I found it refreshing that my son was astute enough to know that whatever was going on with me was *my* problem, not his.

When Kevin was a teenager, he wanted to know how to ask his first girlfriend to the movies. I advised, "Kevin, just ask her like you would your friend John." *Great, a simple answer*, I thought. Moments later, he came up the stairs with pen and paper and asked me to tell him specifically what to say to her. I remember sighing and thinking, *Why does he have to be so perfect at everything? What's wrong with him?* Then it dawned on me that he was nervous and wanted exact wording, and I had brushed him off as if it were no big deal (as my parents had done with me). I should've been grateful that he asked for and valued my opinion. I silently blamed myself for not realizing what he really needed and recognizing that he was scared of being rejected or maybe made fun of.

As a mom, I went back and forth between knowing and guessing what my children were asking and needing—as did my parents, their parents, and so on. There were plenty of times when, after getting angry, pushy, or frustrated and pointing my finger in my children's faces with the "I told you so" attitude, I realized I was wrong. How many times as youngters were we not understood and decided that something was wrong with us instead of realizing that the grown-ups just didn't hear us? As parents, we need to open ourselves to not always being the teacher—we need to be willing to listen and learn from our children too.

If you find yourself in a constant battle with your child and feel as though you cannot get through to each other and are afraid it's too late to fix it, there is hope. **Think about what issues you had with your parents and make a list.**

If your child is old enough, have him make the same list and compare. Do you see similarities? Is anything on his list a surprise to you? If he is too little to make a list, look at your list and see if you recognize your own parenting issues. Is there something you didn't realize you were doing? It may be that you need to go back to chapters 2 and 4, reread your notes, and be honest about how you may be in a childhood loop yourself.

Now ask yourself, What can I change to stop the cycle and repair my relationship with my child or be more open to hearing what he or she may be trying to tell me? For example, did you make your daughter play soccer or cheer because you missed your opportunity and so you are pushing your dreams on her? Can you swallow your pride, admit that you might be wrong, and let her make her own decision?

Once you decide what issues you can work on to repair your relationship, communication will be the key to sustaining an open dialogue with your child. I'm not condoning letting her have her way with everything and being disrespectful; there is still a parent-child role that needs to be maintained. But there is a give-and-take, and once you relax about making mistakes and talk through issues, you will learn to trust your decisions and your instincts.

Nobody is sent home from the hospital with a handbook on child-rearing. Nowadays you can research and read as many books and web-sites as you can stand, but the truth is that each parenting experience is unique, your childhood was one of a kind, and no two children are alike.

Practice going with the flow and taking each issue as it comes. Learn from each other, and be sure to keep an awareness of your own myths and messages. Children are resilient, and as long as you can admit when you're wrong, apologize, and work through

> "We choose listening, learning and loving or we find ourselves listless, lecturing and loathing."
>
> — *Cecilia Tucker*

tough or teaching moments, your patience with each other will grow. Do not try to be perfect with your kids. Be real with them and realize that mistakes will happen.

Listen to what your child needs with your heart, not just your head, and your ability to parent yourself and your children with confidence (and laughter) will get stronger.

And it is true that we don't know what we don't know until we know.

CHAPTER 12

I Didn't See That One Coming—Professional Mistakes

I met a little boy a while back named Jack. Jack has a favorite saying when something catches him off guard. He'll announce with an intense amount of conviction, "Well, I didn't see that one coming!" Being caught unaware is like being caught in your underwear –nobody wants that!

Countless times throughout our lives, we are caught off guard by the missteps we make because we rarely see them coming. Usually our eyes aren't open, or we're in denial. And when we realize the mistake we've made, whether its consequences are long-term or immediate, personal or professional, we break down, hand out blame, and say, "Well, I didn't see that one coming!"

I was friends with the family of a woman who was in a nursing home, and when she passed way, they asked me to officiate at her memorial service. I felt honored to do so. At the wake, I started collecting stories about her. The common themes were that she had a wonderful sense of humor and she liked to dance—in fact, most stories included her dancing. As I wrote the eulogy, I kept thinking of her love for dancing and worked into the speech a funny saying that came from a T-shirt I had that read, "What if the Hokey Pokey *is* what it's all about?"

At the funeral, as I was eulogizing, I spoke about her joyous light and asked, "What if the hoochie-coochie *is* what it's all about?" I realized my mistake immediately as one of the one hundred or so guests spoke up and said, "Don't you mean *Hokey Pokey*?"

"Damn!" came flying out of my mouth, and as soon as I said it, I thought, *Can this get any worse? Now I'm swearing at a funeral.* It felt like professional suicide, yet I had to continue and try to bring dignity back to the service by going forward as if nothing had happened. I felt bad for a while and had to shake it off. I didn't see that one coming. It doesn't sound like a big deal, but it is my profession, and I take it very seriously. Fortunately, the woman's family had her sense of humor. After the service, her son asked me for a copy of it on a CD. I told him that I would get it to him later so that I could edit my mistake, and he replied, "I want it just the way you said it." I tried to convince him to let me edit it, and he refused. With a warm smile he said, "She would've loved it."

Professional mistakes can end a career or just make the day rough, but if you can remember that neither your work nor your mistakes define you, the infractions won't seem so catastrophic. And I've said it before: you need to learn to laugh at your mistakes. If you bury yourself in work because it brings self-worth or to escape reality and avoid knowing yourself, then you will have a very empty life. You will miss feeling the joy of dancing, loving, laughing, and being peaceful. Work is a way to earn a living, but "money don't buy happiness." As a therapist, my services are not cheap, and even those who can afford to see me regularly are in my office for a reason—they are searching for hope and happiness.

One thing we all long for is inner happiness. If we define ourselves by what we do instead of who we are, then what happens when the job is over, the kids are grown, or the spouse leaves or dies? We are caught unaware. One of the saddest parts of my job is when people come to me after giving their entire lives to a career, and they're miserable because they didn't enjoy it at all, and now they're retired and lost. Together we figure out the hours they spent working at something they hated, and it usually works out to about fifty thousand hours! Then I ask them, "Who are you?" I get a blank stare. Then I ask, "How do you enjoy spending your time?" Another blank stare. Then we start working on finding out who they are or want to be outside of their jobs.

The saying about not putting all your eggs in one basket applies here. When that basket is empty, there will be a huge black hole to fill. Unless you know who you are and what you enjoy doing, you will feel listless and maybe depressed or lost. If you expand your horizons and explore life as it happens, find hobbies, spend time with loved ones, and figure out what brings you joy, then you will be fulfilled if that proverbial basket is ever empty. Chances are, if you've done all these things, then you'll have a few baskets with eggs in them, and you won't be staring into that *one* eggless basket.

As life goes on, you can fill several small baskets with new eggs and feel confident that each one is *part* of your life and not your *whole life*. You will know yourself and what brings you happiness, and a new kind of success will be yours. And if you're still in the work world, ask yourself if you like what you do every day. Does it fulfill you? Professionally, we are the most successful when we know who we are and what we like, and when we value time with loved ones. The old saying about work not feeling like work when you're doing the right thing is very true.

Try a new conversation starter the next time you're introduced to someone. Don't ask him what he does for a living; ask him how he likes to spend his time. What a refreshing conversation that becomes.

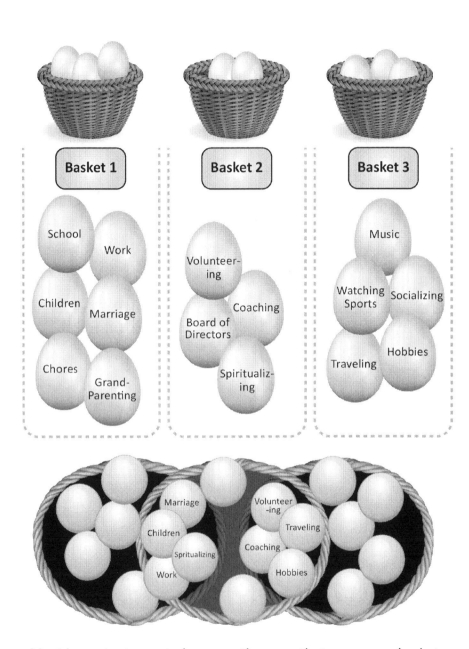

Most important eggs to keep are the ones that cross over baskets.

CHAPTER 13

Recalculating—Stop Blaming; Start Living

I've mentioned that I'm directionally challenged—that cat is out of the bag. So when I was introduced to GPS, I was ecstatic. I thought my problem was solved. Not so much.

I've been through more GPS's than the law should allow. With each new unit, I kept thinking, *When I find the* perfect *one, I will be found.* As I ran through the gamut of GPS's, I felt like Goldilocks: this one is too loud, that one is too confusing, and this one tells me to turn left in the middle of a seven-mile bridge that only goes straight. One can't keep up with the roads and keeps telling me to "please make a U-turn." The next one tells me to turn around, turn around, go back, wrong direction. (Is it just me, or do they start to sound ticked off?) One has a squeaky voice. The next one is too authoritarian for me, and there's the one that's so quiet that even with the volume on the highest level, I can't hear it (kind of like my gut instinct). The last one I wanted to unplug and throw out the window. It took me to places I've never been to take me to places I always go.

Just as I needed those GPS systems to help me navigate the roads, there were times I needed a reliable GPS system to help me navigate life's toughest moments. I recall one of the most distressing times in my life was when I was in seminary. I had gotten involved in a relationship with a man whom I adored. He lifted me out of myself and made me feel special, and I embraced this new, exhilarating phase in my life. It was like inhaling fresh air. I felt like a new me: I had recently lost a lot of weight and was loved by a popular man—so loved that he proposed.

But somewhere during the relationship, my instincts started whispering that something wasn't quite right. After dating for nearly five months, I hadn't been to his house or met any of his friends or family. He was looking at homes for us in Florida to start our new life together, and I felt like the luckiest woman alive. I was so in love, I brushed off my instincts—like so many of us do because we don't want to face what they're warning us about. I didn't want to taint our relationship or make it heavy. I was heading in a direction that was totally new for me, and once again, unknowingly, I was on the wrong road.

One day after our engagement, I was called to the dean's office. I couldn't imagine why, but it's usually not good when you get *the call.* I thought that maybe I had failed a test. The dean started asking personal questions about my relationship while I sat there confused, wondering what this was all about. Finally he stopped beating around the proverbial bush and told me that my fiancé was married and suspected of engaging in illegal activities, though the accusations were unproven. The dean told me this to protect me. He cared about me as a student and didn't want to see me make a mistake. With the speed of light, my life became a discombobulated mess, and I came undone. He was talking about the man I had agreed to spend the rest of my life with.

The dean realized that I was going to need some help getting through the devastation and back on course, so he recommended that I meet with a counselor he knew well. Unfortunately for me, the counselor was across the river in another state, and I had no idea how to get there. With driving directions in hand, I still managed to get lost, *again.* When I finally found him, I announced angrily, "I'm lost!"

"That's why you're here, my dear. That's why you're here," he replied.

After sharing my story with him, I started throwing blame around like Ping-Pong balls. "How could he do this to me and ruin my life? He used me and stomped on my feelings, and I will never be the same! How could I be so stupid and not see that he was hiding something?" Blame, blame, blame.

It's the story of life, isn't it? When we think we have been found, is often when we're most lost. It's easy to blame everyone else for misleading us or for our lack of a lucky break. We aggressively point that first finger as we blame God, the world, or our parents. Sometimes we can have the best GPS in the world and still go the wrong way.

Many of us live our entire lives blaming others for everything that we categorize as *wrong* and never see that we're playing the victim. We're volunteering to be a hostage to the challenges life throws our way and remain blind to the truth.

Along with blaming others, we often blame ourselves. This negative loop destroys our psyche. It puts the brakes on the option to move forward and feel joy in life. We remain a Victim, a Volunteer Hostage, and give up. We keep blaming and slogging through each day feeling helpless.

Hold your hand up. Put all your fingers together as if you're going to wave. Now, separate your fingers between the middle finger and ring finger. You have a V shape. The most important part of the V is what happens in the space or middle. In the middle, you have a voice. Will you be a Valued, Victorious person, or will you choose to be a Volunteer Hostage and Victim?

Conquer Being a Victim of Life and Live a Life of Value

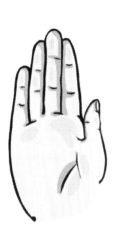

This is where you have Value, Victory and Voice

Your pinky and ring finger are the side of the V that represents feeling Valued and experiencing Victory. Your ring finger is your commitment finger and pretty stable. Sometimes the baby finger strays away from the V—just as you stray away from the things in life that you know are true, good, and just. As the pinky strays and comes back, strays and comes back, it represents being human. Straying and coming back keeps you Valuing the parts of yourself that are beautiful, and it keeps you in Victory mode.

**Commitment to self and
a valued life, stability**

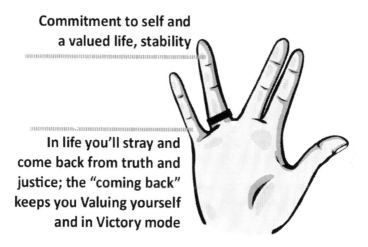

**In life you'll stray and
come back from truth and
justice; the "coming back"
keeps you Valuing yourself
and in Victory mode**

On the other side of the V, you have the first finger, or what's known as the pointer, alongside the middle or bird finger. On this side, you are a Victim or Volunteer Hostage. When life goes awry, you bring out that pointer and poke it at somebody besides yourself; you point and you blame. Then you probably use your middle finger to flip the bird to the world, and we all know what that means. As soon as you point or flip the bird, your thumb comes out as if to hitch a ride, saying, "I'm outta here!"

When life goes awry,
you point and blame,
ignoring a resolution

Once you blame
it's easy to be flippant
with a flippant sign

As soon as you flip the bird,
thumb comes out to hitch a ride
saying, "I'm Outta Here!" and
you run from any truth and value

To stop the cycle of blame, find your truth and relax into the idea that part of being human is that life will always hold challenges; you will never be free from some sort of trial. So how do you get out of the blame rut you're in and become Victorious?

First, recognize and admit that you're blaming someone or something else for your discontent. Stop saying, "I'm here because so-and-so did this or that." Recognize that *you* make the choices you're living with every day. Identify what you need to do to get out of your unhappy situation. I know you're saying, "But I can't because..." Stop using *but* and start asking *how*. How can I make this change? Whatever blaming, binding situation you are in at this very moment is about you and your reaction to it. Take control of that reaction and be truthful; be Victorious. Victory comes from freeing the mind of destructive messages and taking action.

From what situation would you like to be freed? What makes you feel like a Volunteer Hostage?

What would free you from your self-imposed binding situation (i.e., from being a Victim)?

How can you let go of blame and excuses to stay in your new freedom zone and steer clear of being a Volunteer Hostage?

How will you know if you've obtained freedom and truth?

Once you've decided what you need to do, don't talk yourself out of what your gut is telling you. Trust your instincts, and learn to trust others who have your best interest at heart. It is okay to ask for help. Call one of the people from the previous chapters who you felt wouldn't judge you. They can help you see the situation differently, openly, and honestly.

Once you start redirecting your energy by being objective, listening to your gut, talking it through with trusted individuals, and not throwing yourself under a bus, you'll make healthy changes. It is true that success comes from failure. Success also comes from having a plan.

My Plan to Stop Blaming and Start Living

Situation(s) You Want to Change	Excuses	How to Go Forward
For example:	(write them, then cross them off)	
Hate my job	~~*Need the income*~~	*Start networking for a new job* today

When you find yourself at the crossroads of *Victim* or *Victory*, turn down Victory Lane, and you'll see freedom and truth along the way.

CHAPTER 14

Cracked Pipes—Stop Ignoring 'Em and Repair Your Vessel Now

Have you ever had one of those days when everything goes wrong? Many Christmases ago, I got up early to put the finishing touches on dinner before everyone else woke to open gifts. As soon as I started the garbage disposal, I realized it was backed up. Oh, no! This was not happening on a day with hours of cooking ahead, a dozen people staying at our house, and a dozen more on the way. I reset my mind and started using the garbage can instead, continuing with my business.

As guests started waking up and getting ready for the day, my son announced that the toilet was stopped up. I suggested that he just needed to use a plunger, but in the end, it wasn't enough. I began feeling anxious about it and kept listing all the products he could use to unclog it, telling him to keep dumping whatever we could think of down that toilet. After trying and trying and trying some more, we decided not to use it for the day. We closed the door and put a sign on it, pointing potential users to the other two bathrooms.

The morning progressed and more visitors started to show up, so my son thought he had better shower. After a few minutes, he came up from the lower level to the kitchen and mentioned that the shower was draining very slowly. "Okay, don't use that shower," I told him. "Go upstairs instead and use that one." Up he went to try his luck a second time.

Feeling as if I had resolved yet another issue, I continued cooking until another guest came up from the lower level and said, "Something's bubbling up from the shower drain." He said the smell was so foul that we should quarantine the area. I couldn't believe it could be that bad and figured that maybe the dogs had something to do with it. Feeling more frustrated by the minute, I set my cooking aside and went to investigate.

As soon as I reached the bottom step, I could smell the odor, and as I got closer to the bathroom, I noticed the floor was wet. The shower drain was backing sewage up all over the tile floor and into the living area. I lost my patience and felt panic seep in; this floor was where many of our guests were staying, and now it was contaminated—a hazmat situation. Frantically I looked for the plumber's number and felt awful that I had to call him on Christmas Day.

Diagnosis: cracked pipes.

Isn't that the way life happens? When our lives are full of cracked pipes and we feel slightly broken, we wait until the final straw before we act, and then it dawns on us that our problems are much worse than they need to be. We usually think the things that plague us are secrets to those around us, that we can ignore them and they'll disappear. The reality is that our broken parts are pretty obvious to all, and they don't fix themselves.

Most often it takes someone else or a crisis to force us to admit that there's a problem. We've all had a friend or stranger help us with a revelation that illuminates a slight crack, yet it's human nature to wait until the crack becomes a wide crevice. When disaster creeps in, we can either turn away because it's too much hassle and too uncomfortable, or we can use it as an opportunity to evolve.

When your basement is flooded with sewage and you have to call a plumber, it is time to finally admit that if you had acted sooner at the first sign of disaster, you would not be in a state of emergency. It doesn't have to be that way. Throughout this book, you may have thought, *I know there are things wrong, but it's easier to keep plugging away and live with the cracked pipes. I'll hang in there; it'll work itself out, or someone else will fix it.* It's time to change that way of thinking and stop six-monthing through life.

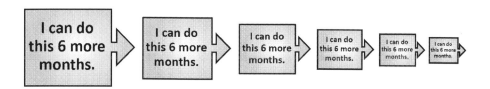

What areas of yourself are you not attending to? Is it your physical health, mental health, or spiritual health?

On the blank picture of a body, note the areas where you know you have cracked pipes and are silently waiting for them to give way. Identify what you're ignoring and face it. Put a name to it.

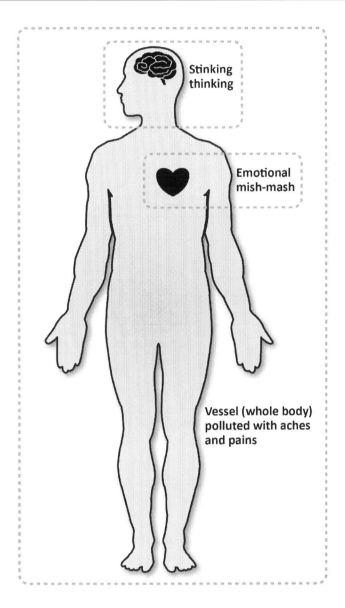

Step out of your comfortable, predictable place into the unpredictable, and repair what needs fixing. You have the tools now to recognize a problem when it's manageable and ask for help before everything gets stopped up, cracks, and floods your world with sewage.

CHAPTER 15

When the Hammock Falls— How to Deal with Life's Blows

One sunny, breezy afternoon, my friend and I were lying crosswise in her hammock, enjoying our iced tea, and talking away when—*bam!*—the strings of the hammock broke, and we were on the ground a split second later. No time to react. For what seemed like thirty minutes, but was probably one, we lay on the ground checking ourselves to make sure we weren't injured, and then the laughing began. We were covered in iced tea and couldn't believe what had just happened. It was a big hammock with substantial ties around an old, thick tree. How could we be swinging away, in a state of pure enjoyment, and have it all end in a split second? That, my friends, is the journey of life.

How many times has this happened to you? It happens to all of us on some level every day, but on a large scale, maybe once or twice in each of our lifetimes.

I see most of my clients when a life crisis gets so bad that they can't see their way through it. They've tried and processed and done all the things people recommend they do, but they're in a state of depression, out of balance, and at times feel like life isn't worth the constant struggle.

Life's crises have nothing to do with God punishing us. Let's clear that up right off the bat. They are part of life's journey. Tough times force us to grow and become better human beings. When my infant daughter died, there was nothing worse. I had already lived through so many tough times that it would've been easy to ask God, *Why me? What did I do?* My grief, guilt, and anger ravaged me for so long that I thought I might not get through it. But I had my faith, and deep inside I trusted that there must be a bigger plan, a positive to this horrible tragedy. Later I learned that our second adopted daughter had been conceived the night that our first daughter died. Wow!

At the time, it may seem impossible that you'll move beyond the sadness or sense of failure as you continue to punish yourself. It is not your fault that your spouse died or that your child is ill or that some other disaster has struck. It is not your fault that you did or didn't do something to make *it* happen. The hammock crashing down was not your fault.

Have you suffered an event that has you in a state of deep self-loathing? Maybe you have pulled inward and find yourself in a very negative place, and now you can't see your way out; you feel hopeless.

Think about the last major ordeal you went through. How did you get through it?

WHEN THE HAMMOCK FALLS—HOW TO DEAL WITH LIFE'S BLOWS

Was there anybody who didn't give up on you, who nurtured you and listened objectively? Do you have anybody now who would catch you if you fell? Write down five people in your life you could turn to and who would listen without judgment. Maybe one or two are the same people you listed from previous chapters.

Did you only come up with two? Then let's start with them. What would happen if you went to them and shared what you're feeling with total honesty? Don't be afraid of judgment—if you wrote down people you can trust, then they won't judge you. Are you willing to let them be a part of your healing process?

Commit to asking *one* person to help, and share your feelings with that person. Reach out. Ask him or her over for a visit, or meet for coffee. Discuss what's happening—what's *truly* happening. Don't hold back. Healing is a community commitment, not an individual journey. People who love us want to help us, so let them.

Once you've reached out, you will be amazed at the sudden lightness you feel when you accept that you don't have to go through it alone. You will experience massive relief and feel unburdened.

Now that you've taken the very important first step and reached out, find a direction that's going to take you to your goal. Choose one thing from the *How to Go Forward* list in chapter 12 and focus on *one* action. Meanwhile, to lift your fog of sadness or worry, on a loose sheet of paper or a sticky note, make a daily gratitude list of the beauty around you, and keep it where you'll see it throughout the day (e.g., at your desk or in the kitchen). The list might look like this:

- Tulips by the front door opened today, and they're two bright colors.
- My favorite movie is on tonight, and Sarah is coming over to watch it with me.
- Tomorrow is Saturday, and I get to sleep in.
- Mom called this morning, and she's feeling much better.

Even if it's just two things that will bring you joy, focus on them for thirty seconds and smile.

If you sit at a desk all day looking down at your computer, make sure you raise your head and look up every few minutes. You'll automatically take in your surroundings and halt your self-absorption. You can't help it. Try it. Look up and out the window or around the room. What do you see? Did you forget about your blues just then? It works!

If you can rearrange your desk so that your monitor or laptop is up at eye level, it will change your brain chemistry, and you'll feel better without even knowing why.

Get a new hammock, hang it in the tree, and sway without fear. Don't worry that it'll fall again or that you'll miss out on those relaxing, glorious moments of life. Even if they're fleeting, they are worth highlighting and experiencing. Each day will inevitably contain positive events along with incidents that challenge you to the core, but it is how you choose to react to those incidents that shapes your journey through life.

CHAPTER 16

Chinese Cat-Santa— The Right Person at the Right Time

There are times in life when we say, "I don't need anybody. I'm tired of others giving me what *they* want instead of what *I* need." We reflect back on all the times that someone has taken advantage of us, taken us for granted, or duped us. Many times we've loved somebody only to be hurt by him or her, and though the situation may change, the outcome is always the same: we don't get what we need from that other person and end up hurt.

One year we invited a family friend to the house for our Christmas celebration. When she arrived, she had a small gift for us. After thanking her, we put it under the tree to be opened later and continued on to dinner. Shortly after she left, we decided that we couldn't wait to open the gift, so we gathered around and tore open the wrapping. Much to our surprise, it was a little bobblehead figurine that looked like a Chinese Cat-Santa. Huh? For a minute, we all just looked at each other with confusion as the head bobbed and swayed to the Chinese tune it was playing. Not one of us is Chinese. What on earth was she thinking? We looked at the box again to see what we were missing and to decipher if it was a Chinese cat or a Santa. (If it was a cat, it sure was different from any cat I'd ever seen.) The more we fooled with this little gift, the more we laughed and interacted. We made it play its song over and over and bobble its head. We were in fits of laughter by the time we put it away much later into the evening.

As the holiday went on, I kept looking at the gift and chuckling and, of course, telling my other friends about it, sharing the laughter. I figured there must be something about it that brought good luck, and I took it to another party on New Year's Eve. I introduced it around as if it were a family member, and it continued to bring joy and laughter to everyone I shared it with. This little Chinese Cat-Santa gifted dozens more people with belly laughs. Another friend asked me if she could have it to take to a white elephant party, so I gave it to her, and she sent me photos of it bringing joy to many others. What a lucky gift! That Chinese Cat-Santa has been to more parties and bestowed laughter on more people than my friend ever imagined, and it is probably still out there carousing at holiday parties.

Probably one of the most ridiculous gifts I have ever received became one of the most important lessons I have ever learned. Just because you get something you don't want and may not see the point in it, that doesn't mean it's not what you need at the time. Laughter and joy, bringing people together, and good luck all resulted from a strange toy that I never would've chosen.

Just as in life, when we don't think we need anything or anybody, or when we don't see the point in what we're going through or what we're getting from others, we need to look deeper. Sometimes the most unusual things bring us together; sometimes it's not what we asked for at all, yet there it is. Many times the people in our lives are our silent, unexpected gift, while others become the very thing we need to let go of. The grace of people coming in and out of our lives and leaving behind cherished memories and lessons learned—some good and others challenging—brings growth.

When was the last time you said, "I don't need *nothing or nobody* because nothing you're giving me is what I want, and you are not what I am looking for"? If someone gifts you with trail mix full of nuts, don't just say, "I don't hike, and I don't eat nuts." Tell the gift giver thank you, and pick out the pieces of the trail mix that you like (while "hiking" on the couch). Maybe the dried fruit is in there because your blood sugar is dropping but you aren't aware of it, and when you eat it, you feel better.

Make a list of all the things in your life that you've received but never asked for or wanted. Next to those, write the positive outcomes associated with each of them.

Now make that same list using people in your life that you did not want to be there. What did they give you? How did they change your life for better or worse?

Lastly, write down something about yourself that you wish was not a part of your character. How has it served you in a positive way to be the person you have become?

Things Received
For example:
Promotion that I didn't want

Positives

Learning new ideas, earning more money

People in My Life
For example:
Susan

Change for Better or Worse

Realize how lucky I am in my marriage

My Unwanted Characteristics Positive Outcome
For example:
Intense, hard on myself

Never give up on my dreams

Living the life of "I don't need nothing or nobody" will not bring joy, laughter, or luck. It will bring just the opposite—loneliness, depression, and trials. Open your mind and heart and be thankful for unexpected, unwanted people and events in your life. Embrace the Chinese Cat-Santas that come along. Sometimes the most unwanted thing in the universe or the most unwanted person on the planet is just right for where you are right now.

CHAPTER 17

Grateful Givers—The Key to Successful Relationships

Not long ago I was sitting on a plane, crammed into a seat that seems to get smaller every time I fly. It's nearly impossible *not* to get to know your "neighbor" on a plane, so a conversation started between me and the young man to my right. We exchanged pleasantries, and I learned that he was engaged to be married. After a few minutes of conversation, he said, "Given the fact that you're a minister and a therapist, can I ask you a question?" Sure enough, he asked the age-old question: "What's the secret to a long, happy marriage?"

At first I wanted to give him a funny answer like "separate bathrooms and closets," but I could tell he wanted a real answer, so I pondered for a few minutes and summed it up for him. "The happiest relationships are found when both people are grateful givers."

He looked at me a little puzzled. "I call it the attitude of gratitude," I explained. "When both people are loving and give to each other and others daily, whether it is moral support, a hug, or a simple act of kindness, there is joyfulness in the relationship. If one person is a taker or is not a gracious receiver, it will cause problems."

In order to be a grateful giver, it's important to walk that fine line between being a giver and knowing how to receive versus being a doormat. Many of you may be in one-sided relationships and probably think it's your duty to always be the giver—even if it's not reciprocated. Those relationships are toxic. Resentment builds, self-esteem plummets, and the give-and-take becomes give, give, give, while the other person takes, takes, takes. Let me assure you that eventually these habits will create a wedge so deep that it will become toxic to you, the Giver. You will start to feel taken for granted but won't speak up for yourself; you'll just keep giving. Then after a while, you'll feel worthless, depressed, and angry. Maybe you'll start verbally lashing out or self-abusing instead. Now, in place of the love you felt for the other person, you'll look at him or her with different eyes and will feel hopeless and stuck.

It's decision time. If you are a Giver in a relationship with a Taker, now is the time to tip the balance, pioneer your new self, and feel appreciated. If you are sure that talking about it with the Taker won't change anything, if his wounds are so deep that he is hardwired to take and doesn't see what's wrong, then you can start to make small changes to regain your sense of self. Either leave him or learn how to stand up for yourself and do what you need to do to stop being a victim.

Start by taking tiny steps to feel gratitude, or give to someone who will really appreciate it. Tomorrow or even today, make eye contact with your cashier at the grocery store, ask about her day, and genuinely listen and respond. Or open a door for an elderly person. You will be rewarded with true gratitude, and that thankfulness will give you joy and hope.

Next time you're tempted to put aside your needs for the needs of a Taker, stop! Think about the worst thing that can happen if you put your needs first. For example, if your Taker asks you for a ride home after she drops her car off for an oil change, but you've worked all day and helping her out means you'll miss your gym time for the third day in a row, how will you feel? You'll probably be mad at yourself for missing another workout, and mad at the Taker for expecting you to sacrifice your time, once again, for her needs. If you say politely, "I'm sorry, I have an appointment that I can't miss today. Maybe we can arrange another time, or you can ask someone else," the result will be that the Taker does exactly what you ask her to do, and you get to be true to your needs. She may be surprised by your new behavior, but she will eventually come to respect it. If that never happens, then you will need to assess the true nature of the relationship, and decide if you want to continue with it or end it.

Make a list of people you give to who are always grateful.

Now make a list of those you give to regularly who take advantage of your giving.

Make a list of the times you stood up for yourself and set boundaries.

Now decide whether you want to keep those Takers in your life. If setting boundaries with them doesn't work, it's okay to let them go. It will be hard to do, but as each day passes and you're no longer routinely being taken advantage of, your joy will increase, and the grateful receivers in your life will notice. You will transform into a joyful Giver once again.

Giving completes our purpose for each day. When we come home, we tend to share the good stuff, and that brings positive energy and love to the relationships around us.

CHAPTER 18

Love for All—Includers and Excluders

You just read the section on Grateful Givers, and we touched on Takers. Let's take that a step further and explore what makes a person a Taker and how it can disrupt your happiness. We'll replace *giving* and *taking* with *including* and *excluding*.

Thanksgiving dinner at our house has been a melting pot for many years. A couple years ago, our daughter looked around the dinner table and felt inspired by the group of people that I was proud to call friends and family. We were blessed with an abundance of food, and the conversations flowed.

Around our table sat a Mexican person, a black man, a biracial newborn, Caucasian people, youngsters, hipsters, a ninety-year-old, and a gay person. There was also a Jewish person, Christians, vegans, people of large and small stature, conservatives, and fundamentalists. Some were family, some were friends—and all were equal in our house.

It has always been natural for our family to include everyone, to sit free of judgment, and to be open-minded. We embrace all traditions that are different from ours and welcome those differences. That

Thanksgiving we all learned new things about each other and held deep gratitude for the love shared. This is inclusiveness: no judgment, and love for all.

On the other hand, we all know adults who act like children and exclude others by not reaching out, not giving, being suspicious of kindness, and always wanting their needs met before others'. This may work at three years of age, but not at thirty. Whether it is a friend, a sibling, a parent, or a spouse, being in a relationship with an Excluder is self-defeating.

I often see the struggle in a marriage when an Excluder wants to be the center of his spouse's world, and he goes to great lengths to make sure his spouse is *all* his—for example, having few outside friends or hobbies without his spouse.

Excluders learned their behavior as children. They often felt like burdens because their parents were too busy to spend time with them, ignored them, and didn't reach out and love them enough, or because their parents were Excluders themselves. As kids, Excluders act out and try to be the center of attention yet push others away. This becomes a pattern that continues into adulthood. They get into trouble, lack hope, and see no humor in life.

Excluders go through life pushing people away out of fear. *Fear* is the big motivator for these people: fear of rejection, abandonment, not being good enough, and not finding anyone to love them. Eventually, the Excluder will find an Includer to love, and that person becomes her everything. The Excluder will take and take and take from the Includer, but it will never be enough to prove she is loved.

Includers are easy targets for Excluders because they can be giving to a fault. They're not great with boundaries and always put others before themselves and their own needs. They are usually kindhearted and compassionate, which is like a magnet for Excluders. They will give and give and give of themselves to try to lift up the Excluder until they have nothing left of their sense of self, few friends, and few social outlets.

Your answers to the questions below will indicate if you are being kind and generous or being a doormat for an Excluder.

- Do you let an Excluder dictate your schedule?
- Do you fear judgment when you don't do something the way an Excluder demands?
- Does the Excluder make you feel guilty or exaggerate an illness or injury when you go out to enjoy time with friends or family?
- Do you try to stop having your own opinions and interests because it's easier than fighting with an Excluder?
- Does your self-esteem disappear a little each day, and does getting through each of those days feel heavy?
- Is being around an Excluder a bummer, but you can't seem to avoid it?

Did you answer *yes* to any or all of these? Are you assessing a relationship as you read this and thinking, *Oh, no! That's me*? It usually takes a major life event to admit what's happening and start making changes. It will take a while to undo the damage and regain enough self-esteem to make important changes. But we can do this together.

Whether the Excluder is a friend, family member, or romantic partner, the same rules apply as you try to disassociate; the only difference is that with a friend or romantic partner, you can sever ties. Start by separating what's about you and what's about him or her. Realize that the Excluder has a social problem that stems from a childhood issue. It is not about you. What is about you is the way you react to the situation.

Don't be mean or cruel; see the situation for what it is and change what you can. For example, leave the room when the Excluder's attitude or demands become too much. If she points out an imperfection that you know you have or are insecure about, acknowledge it and move on. Say something like, "I know; I am working on that. Thanks for reminding me." If you get mad, you're giving the Excluder what she wants—a reaction. The Excluder wants to hurt you and appear superior. If you're agreeable, it diffuses the situation immediately.

If the Excluder is demanding and asks you to do chores or activities that you're not comfortable with, politely decline and remove yourself from the situation temporarily. For example, if the Excluder asks you over for dinner, but the next thing you know, he or she is asking you to bring most of the food, simply state that you don't have extra time right now and suggest that the dinner be moved to a date when both parties can contribute equally.

Keep in mind that if this person is family, you want to leave each situation with no regrets. It will challenge every fiber of your being stand your ground with the Excluder and still be kind. Being nice yet firmly stating your wishes or opinions, you are taking charge by shutting off the negativity and turning it to your advantage. You end up being the bigger person.

Yes, the Excluder will push back and may strike harder at first. Be strong, stand your ground, and reinforce it with positivity. I'm not saying to reward his or her behavior; just take charge of your feelings and your reactions. It will be difficult and will require practice. You will notice that if you don't argue or act offended, the Excluder will have no reply. He or she will simply move on to the next poor soul, and you will not be a victim anymore. When you start feeling guilty, keep these points in mind:

- Remember, it is not your problem. It is truly *not* about you; it's about his or her issues.

- Change what you can—your reaction to action—and remove yourself from the environment if possible.
- If you're not a player in the game, there is no game.

Practicing these behaviors will stop you from being a target of abuse. If you stay in the relationship, once you get to a place where his or her exclusiveness doesn't affect you quite as much, try to reinforce the situation with kindness or even love if you can. For example—and this may be a stretch, but it is worth a try eventually—sign a birthday card using "Love, _____."

Being an Includer is a wonderful way to go through life if you can learn these important steps to being a realistic Giver. Be kind to yourself, and keep your own needs a priority. I'll see you at the crossroads of *victim* and *valued*.

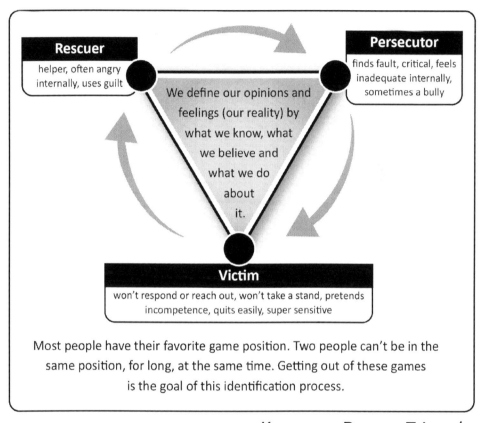

Rescuer
helper, often angry internally, uses guilt

Persecutor
finds fault, critical, feels inadequate internally, sometimes a bully

We define our opinions and feelings (our reality) by what we know, what we believe and what we do about it.

Victim
won't respond or reach out, won't take a stand, pretends incompetence, quits easily, super sensitive

Most people have their favorite game position. Two people can't be in the same position, for long, at the same time. Getting out of these games is the goal of this identification process.

Karpman Drama Triangle
Adapted from Relationship and Management by Lewis Guine, LCSW

CHAPTER 19

All about SSSSelf—How to Avoid the Narcissistic Snare

"Oh, she's so sweet, and she's always the life of the party." Each of us has probably heard similar praise about a person we know well, but we feel we're crazy because the person in question annoys us and tries our patience. Well, we're not crazy. The general public that is in love with our friend, the narcissist, doesn't know her well enough to see the true person behind the façade. Our narcissist doesn't know herself either, since hiding behind a public image and becoming whomever she needs to be in the moment defines her existence.

It's ironic that I'm writing a chapter in this book about narcissists—wouldn't they love that? But there is good reason. We've all been snared by one and have had our lives negatively affected by him or her. We're trusting by nature and can't believe that someone could be so self-absorbed, so we continually think it must be us and not him or her.

Narcissistic people are charming, the life of the party, and always engaging. When you're developing a friendship with a narcissist, he will show an interest in your life and appear to be a good listener. He will be there for your every need and will show empathy for any situation you may be dealing with. Then the relationship slowly evolves and becomes all about him. The transition is so smooth that at first it seems like you have so much in common, but in reality he is agreeing with you and then minimizing your experience.

Let's say you share a painful childhood memory. As you're telling the story, your narcissistic friend says, "Oh, I know what you're going through. I'm sorry to hear that. But look at you now. And by the way, you'll never guess what I just did!" The focus will be back on him, and your story is just a blip on his radar. It doesn't sink in at the time how dismissive he is toward you. You think you're being praised for what you've endured, when in reality you have found someone who will constantly belittle you, one-up you, and need to be the top dog in every situation.

The narcissist will create an environment that's all about him no matter what. And that personal story you shared? It'll crop up later at an inappropriate time, maybe as a joke at a party, or it will even be used to the narcissist's advantage.

Let's say your new narcissistic friend is a woman. As you grow to know her, you realize that her outward behavior is disrespectful (e.g., she ignores you at every party in order to go work the room), and she will often make fun of something you're sensitive about in front of others. You start to see that her sense of humor is often at the expense of others, and she embellishes her stories to weave intricate webs of lies.

Increasingly you'll be annoyed by her need to be the center of attention as she shows up late for every date or appointment while you sit there waiting for her, or *you're* late to every event because of her. Once the honeymoon phase is over, she can't be bothered to be there when you need her, unless it fits her agenda and makes her look like a hero. Unreliability and lying will become commonplace. Yet there you are, still friends.

Eventually, tired of the drama, the letdowns, feeling small, and having your feelings hurt, you'll have an *aha!* moment. You'll recognize that you're the only consistent friend standing by the narcissist, since most of her relationships only last until her newest buddy finds out the real deal and drops her, or she doesn't get the desired ego stroking.

Most often, trying to slip from a narcissist's grasp is tough. As soon as you make up your mind and begin to change your behavior, it's as if she senses your dissension and reels you back in with a random act of kindness, or tells you, "I don't know what I'd do without you." The narcissist becomes delightful and boosts your ego, and suddenly you're glad you're still friends—until you realize, once again, that she is a devil in a red dress.

This seesaw relationship will go on for a while, sometimes for years, until you find self-respect and take action. Being subtle with a narcissist does not work. When you share your hurt feelings face-to-face or mention that you've grown tired of her disregard, at first she will listen and apologize or buy you something nice. Then she will turn around and do the very thing you're upset about because a narcissist *does not get it*. Time and again you will express frustration while trying to get her to understand until eventually she'll get angry and turn it back on you. She'll say things like, "Don't be so sensitive," or "I'm sorry you feel that way," and then you'll feel punished again.

Who do you know that fits this description?

Maybe it is your mother, father, or sibling. Maybe it's your spouse, business partner, or best friend. Knowing how to handle this complicated personality is vital for self-preservation.

Please read this very carefully: narcissists prey on kind people who they know will be good for them. They pick up on a little weakness in your self-confidence that they can manipulate. If this happens over and over again in your relationships, guess what these relationships have in common? *You.* Maybe it's time to figure out whatever it is in you that is a magnet for narcissists, and then demagnetize it.

What strings are attached to the supposed benefits of these relationships? If the narcissist buys you things or introduces you in high society, are you obligated to be there every time he needs favors or 3:00 a.m. interventions? Are you expected to do his dirty work or take his verbal abuse when it suits him? When you tell him something good has happened to you, does he act jealous and make fun of it or tear it down so you're convinced it wasn't that great after all?

Write down what it is that you think draws narcissists to you. What is your hook? For example, are you rarely social and don't get invited out? With a narcissist, you get to be social and regarded as one of the in crowd. Maybe the narcissist is wealthy and you're not, so he or she lavishes you with goods you wouldn't otherwise have. Or maybe the narcissist chose you because you're steadfast and well known, and he or she needs *your* connections to feel bigger than before. Don't forget, narcissists are extremely insecure and seek constant reassurance that they are worthy.

My Hook or Insecurity	Benefit to Being His/ Her Friend	Cost
For example: *Introverted*	*Socializing with safety net, having fun*	*Made fun of for the sake of entertainment*

Once you've identified the need that the narcissist is filling for you, ask yourself who else can fill that need in a healthy way. Look to your true friend who is always there, never asks for anything in return, and treats you with respect. This will show you the difference between the narcissist's tainted, self-serving idea of love and true friendship.

Healthy People in My Life

What can you do to stop falling prey to the narcissist's tease of truth? Firmly decide that you're tired of the hurt and drama and start to back away. Reduce your time socializing and talking with her every time she calls or texts, and stop being there every time she needs a favor. That's the hardest one. When she needs you, you feel like a bad, selfish person if you don't help because she's been there for you. But has she?

When did I need my narcissistic friend, but he or she wasn't there for me?

If you're dealing with a family member, a boss, or someone you can't eliminate from your life, make a list of boundaries to start enforcing. For example, when you meet with your narcissist, keep it short, don't offer up a lot of personal information (though you may be bursting to share a new development), and act as if he's an acquaintance. There's no need to be rude, just a bit aloof. If it's your spouse, managing your reaction and altering your goals for the relationship will get you by, but unless the relationship ends, you will lead a very stressful life.

When you are obligated to have lunch or be together, keep your expectations low. If you hope that he will be on time *just this once* or that you'll finally have a truthful heart-to-heart, be warned: do not have *any* expectations. Remind yourself that he will be late and loud to make sure he is seen. Remember, the conversation will be shallow and all about him, so prepare to listen to the chatter. When you look at the situation objectively by taking your emotions out of it, your stress level will decrease, you'll stop trying to impress, and you'll gain confidence you didn't know you had.

Narcissist	Boundaries	Do not expect...	Ways to Not Fall Prey
For example: Brad	*Keep personal stories out of it.*	*Him to be on time.*	*Don't give details if he asks about personal life.*

When narcissists sense that you're slipping from their coils but you still feel vulnerable to their charms, ask yourself how you feel after an encounter. Here are some examples:

- Tense
- Not heard
- Placated
- Worn-out
- Put in your place
- Humored

Just to be clear, narcissists differ from excluders in many ways. The dynamics may feel similar, but if you remember from the previous chapter, excluders exclude outwardly rather than include everybody as if they're best friends. Narcissists are takers who don't act as if they're taking; excluders make no bones about it. Narcissists are warm and act as if they're the friendliest and most inclusive people in the world, while excluders are cold and disdainful.

The Mayo Clinic defines *narcissism* as "a mental disorder in which people have an inflated sense of their own importance, a deep need for admiration, and a lack of empathy for others. But behind this mask of ultra-confidence lies a fragile self-esteem that's vulnerable to the slightest criticism." Narcissism is a choice to gain love and attention, usually made in childhood between the ages of two and five, and it becomes a way of life, a personality type. Behavior therapy rarely changes narcissists because they don't recognize any need to change and refuse to believe that they are, in fact, narcissistic, even when they've lost a job or a marriage and are alone in the world.

In today's world, narcissists have the benefit of technology to enable them to be seen and heard 24-7. It's called social media, and it's getting easier every minute to have their pictures or selfies out in the world for countless people—including strangers—to see. Their egos soar as the comments come in about how attractive they look or how many Likes their posts get. Any attention or recognition is affirmation, and it's immediate, although usually insincere. *Who cares* what they eat daily for breakfast or where they're dining! A sure way to know if you've friended a narcissist is if he or she is a chronic advertiser of every move.

Once you decide to step away, whether completely or partially, you will miss your narcissist. You will miss the fun times and the laughter and be tempted to go back again. Stay strong and turn your attention to your other friends, or reach out and make a new friend who gives you healthy love and support. Eventually you will miss the narcissist less and less and feel relieved to be free from his or her daily demands. You may look back on the fun times fondly, but always remind yourself of the drama, the hurt, the embarrassment, and the dread that came with each encounter. You'll find yourself saying, "It's not worth it," and you'll know you are free from his or her snares.

CHAPTER 20

The Rearview Mirror—Regrets

Driving down the street one day, I found myself looking in the rearview mirror as I was moving forward. It's pretty hard to move forward when you're looking backward, and just as I realized my error, I crashed into the car in front of me. I'd had several close calls up to that point doing the very same thing, looking to the left, to the right, and behind me as I was moving forward.

One time I was driving a bit too fast on a curvy road, and as I crested the hill, I encroached on the center line as another car approached. The words "Shit, man!" flew out of my mouth, blaming the other driver. I narrowly missed the other car, and my passenger laughed and asked why I blamed the other guy. I tried to make up something that he had done wrong, but the truth is that I had been going way too fast on the wrong side of the road. "Shit, man" kind of describes what it's like when I find myself spending way too much time looking left, right, and behind me, hogging more than my share of the road, and going too fast. I often forget that every time I drive, there is a large window showing a panoramic view of what's in front of me, what lies ahead.

It is very common to find ourselves looking back over our shoulders, to the left, or to the right rather than focusing on the future—on what's out front. I'm not suggesting that we ignore the past; it has made us who we are. The past is a guide, a map for the future. We gain wisdom and learn how to let go of our pain and become stronger so that we can embrace our todays.

It has been said that if you have one foot in the past and one foot in the future, you'll find yourself urinating on today. Not a pleasant picture, but think about it for a minute. Living in a place that's not the present creates regrets and if onlys. Letting yesterday's regrets, tomorrow's dreams, and foolish pride control today keeps us in a state of denial, of not admitting to and dealing with our disappointments. This cycle creates shame—not guilt, shame. You wake up one day and ask yourself, *Where did all the time go?* Then you realize that you've been living each day looking back and muttering *if only*, or dreaming of a day that isn't here yet, wishing and squandering the minutes of the present day. The shame comes from feeling bad about yourself as a person—not about what you did or didn't do, but about who you've become and the lack of personal growth.

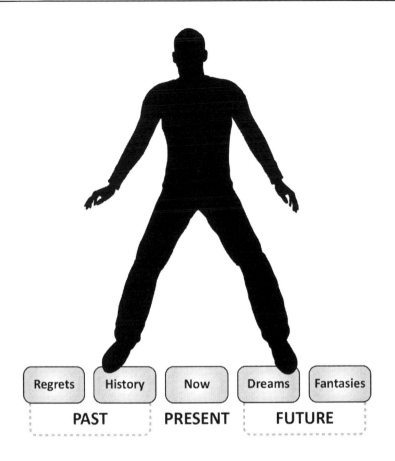

Regrets will keep you up at night; they'll eat at you so you're even less able to deal with your emotions and move forward. Regrets include not just your own life choices but also times when you didn't say, "I release you." There is no rewind button on your days. You can't go back and say or do things differently. So how do you move forward and keep living for today while at the same time letting go of your regrets? Start by setting pride aside, admitting what the regrets are, and writing them down.

What are your regrets?

Are any of these currently affecting your life? Can you fix any of them? Can you forgive someone or say you're sorry? Can you make a job or marriage change? If there is a way to mend, change, fix, repair, or right a wrong, then do it today.

What if the regret is something that can't be repaired or undone? Start practicing forgiveness. Forgive yourself, and hold yourself accountable to learn from the mistake and not repeat it. Maybe someone died before you had a chance to say, "I love you," and now it's too late. It may seem an insurmountable task to move beyond the heartbreak of your own regret, but with time and forgiveness, the regret will diminish, and you'll be able to move beyond it. Sometimes it helps to confess your regrets out loud to a trusted loved one. Saying it out loud releases the guilt and stops the closed loop of self-berating chatter. The shame and agony you've held in secret will lessen, and healing will begin. If your regret involves someone else, writing an unsent letter to that person helps you take ownership of the regret and helps you put your pride aside and stare your regret in the face. If the regret is solely yours, you can write yourself a letter as well. Confess, ask for forgiveness, forgive yourself, change what you can, and don't let future regrets go unaddressed.

Look at your regrets list again. What hurdles have kept you from making changes? Is it laziness, pride, denial, being overwhelmed, or not knowing where to begin?

WHO NEEDS A DAMN THERAPIST ANYWAY?

What is the worst thing that will happen if you admit you were wrong or if you make this change?

If your regret can be made better, how can you get started on changing it today?

In order to realistically keep moving forward with your life goals and dreams without living only for tomorrow, it helps to make a list of those goals like you did in chapter 7. Identify small daily or monthly actions you can take to reach those goals rather than saying, "Someday I will..." Start doing something to get there. For example, if you want to retire in three years, but your house payment is keeping you from doing that, put a little extra into your house payment for a while. It may require giving up your boutique-coffee habit or something else to get there, but if it helps you reach your goal, there will be no regrets when retirement comes early.

Goals and dreams for your future:

Steps you can take *now* to reach those goals:

Remember, the window of life is like a thirty-eight-foot RV windshield. You can see directly in front of you and for miles out in front. But if you look out the back window or in the rearview mir-

> "I can choose to be happy now....Or I can try to be happy When....Or If..."
>
> **— from the Precious Present,**
>
> **Spencer Johnson**

ror, even in a huge RV, you can only see a small sliver of what's behind. Looking back only serves as a reference—it doesn't get you where you need to go. Looking at the immediate future and then down the road a little way helps you plan your route safely. Free yourself from your regrets about your past and fantasies about your future, and start living in the moment.

CHAPTER 21

Bitter versus Better—Forgive and Let Go

It was my day off, and I had been looking forward to spending time with my two-year-old daughter, Kristin. She and I spent the day running errands and then picked up her brother from school and ordered pizza for dinner. Around five thirty, Kristin started not feeling well. Her brother, Kevin, had been sick recently, so I figured it was just a touch of what he had, but I thought I'd put a call in to the doctor to be safe. She didn't have a fever, and the on-call doctor didn't call me back right away, but I watched Kristin closely. Finally, when the doctor called at seven o'clock, she only said to keep an eye on Kristin, and if she worsened, I should take her to the walk-in clinic in the morning. Feeling reassured, I put Kristin to bed around nine o'clock.

As I was readying for bed at about ten forty-five, I checked on my daughter. My heart sank—she was as yellow as a squash and red-hot to the touch. Her temperature was 104 degrees, and she had a bloated stomach. My husband and I rushed her to the emergency room in record time. The staff was slow to triage and didn't get her into a room until around midnight. Her heart stopped at twelve thirty. They revived her, but Kristin coded two more times and then died within minutes.

The doctor on call that night didn't get there until Kristin had already coded. We found out later that our adopted baby girl had a pin-hole in her diaphragm from birth. It had ruptured and leaked stomach acid into her lungs. Neither the doctor nor the hospital staff provided the proper care that night, and our baby was gone. As you can imagine, there are no words for the agony, the grief, the anger, the guilt. This was a turning point in my life in many ways. Mainly I realized what I can control and what I cannot.

We learned a short time later that the doctor who had treated Kristin had been abusing substances regularly and had done so that night. I worked through the myriad of crushing emotions for many, many years until eventually I felt as though I could forgive her. I started praying for the doctor, feeling that I had come a long way. What I realized a couple of years later was that, at the end of those prayers for her, there was always a PS: *And never let her forget what she did to my child, so she'll never do it to another.* Closing a prayer of forgiveness with a PS is not truly forgiving.

As a society, we aren't taught how to forgive. Kids are told to say they're sorry or accept another's apology without understanding why. We are often made to feel as though our feelings aren't valid, and we're not given the skills to know how to truly forgive. It does not come naturally, and simply saying, "I forgive you" is not the same as forgiving. Forgiveness is a process, not a one-time act of letting go. It is something we do for ourselves, not for others. When we forgive completely, we stop feeling ill will toward the one who hurt us. It is a conscious decision of kindness and goodwill toward a person who we feel doesn't deserve it.

With forgiveness, eventually you will feel compassion for the wrongdoer and find resolution to your grief, pain, and loss. Without forgiveness, the person who has wronged you takes up unnecessary space in your head and drains positive energy. Lack of forgiveness or holding a grudge will eat the healthy cells that make you a strong person. There is scientific proof that not forgiving negatively affects your cardiovascular and nervous systems.

Toxic emotions stop you from moving forward, and the hurt stays with you and shadows each day with a little cloud of powerlessness. You may not notice it's happening. You may say, "Oh, that was so many years ago; I've let it go." But ask yourself, have you forgiven? Have you freed that person and incident from your mind and come to peace with it without anxiety or anger bubbling up whenever you think about it? Chances are, probably not.

Try to remember that the person who wronged you is a human being. Also remember, at one time or another, *you* have hurt someone unintentionally, or even intentionally. No one is immune to hurting others. The person you are struggling to forgive has his own problems to deal with and may have unresolved childhood issues that explain his behavior. He may be spiteful, vengeful, childish, power hungry, manipulative, mean, sarcastic, or bossy. He may have hurt you in so many ways over the years that you can't imagine forgiving him. But he doesn't need to know. It has nothing to with an apology, nor does it have anything to do with reconciliation. If reconciliation happens, that's wonderful. But more times than not, forgiveness is one-sided. Forgive and let it go.

Learning to let go means that you realize you can't control or fix other people. Letting go means that you learn from the incident, which inspires growth. Letting go means you stop judging and instead, let others control their own destinies. Ultimately, letting go is living fully in the present, knowing there is a future without the hurt. Letting go doesn't mean you stop caring, but you fear less and give it up to your God. You cannot control everything and everyone. You can only control *your* actions and thoughts. If you decide it's time to forgive another, look at what you've learned along the way, dig deep, and find grace. Grace is the unmerited gift of God.

Let me be clear about something else: forgiving is not forgetting. Forgetting may do just as much harm as holding a grudge because you're burying your true feelings about the wrongdoing. Forgetting usually leads to suppressing and denying and then ultimately to emotional and physical turmoil years later. Processing the hurt is healthy. Feel it, work through it for as long as it takes, and then let the forgiving and healing begin. There is no right or wrong time; it may take years. But as long as you're allowing the process to happen, the forgiveness will happen too.

Forgiving is not about condoning, absolving, self-sacrificing, or swallowing your true feelings, nor is it a clear-cut decision. It is not isolated to an act of Christian faith. Forgiveness is part of being human and offering up mind, body, and soul. It is an experience of serenity that all humans seek, regardless of religion. It is an internal healing process, a discovery after the fact, a sign of positive self-esteem, and a recognition that the past is holding you back. It is when you no longer want others to suffer and realize that punishing them doesn't heal you.

If you need to forgive yourself, follow the same guidelines as above and let it go. Realize you're human. Stop having regrets about things you can't undo, change the things you can, stop living in the past, and look forward to every day. Give up trying to mold your feelings into what you think they should be, and let your feelings be true. Feel what you need to feel and move on.

More and more research is showing that people with forgiving spirits are less depressed and have more friends, longer marriages, closer relationships, fewer stress-related health issues, better immune systems, lower blood pressure, and less heart disease. Wow! Do we need any other reasons to forgive and be merciful?

FORGIVENESS IS NOT AN ACTION

Forgiveness happens naturally with confronting your feelings and moving on within daily life.

Forgiveness is a discovery, not something done.

Forgiving is not:
- Forgetting
- Condoning
- Absolution
- A form of self-sacrifice
- Swallowing true feelings and pride
- A clear-cut one-time decision

Forgiving is:
- A by-product of an ongoing healing process
- Internal process
- Sign of a positive self-esteem
- Letting go of intense emotions from events of the past
- Recognizing the past holding you back
- No longer wanting others to suffer as you have
- Realizing punishing them doesn't heal you
- Putting energy elsewhere in a more positive direction

Two falsehoods about forgiving:
- Forgiving is not about forgetting
- Forgiving is not condoning or excusing the tragedy

FORGIVENESS IS A DISCOVERY AFTER THE FACT.

— Adapted from Louis Smedes, Forgive & Forget

CHAPTER 22

Except for the Part Where Grandma Died—Be Comfortable in Your Story

One of my funniest memories is of working with my mother to help her prepare for her own funeral. She had specific ideas about what she liked and did not like and wanted to fully contribute to her own final salute.

Several years prior to her death at age eighty-eight, my brother informed me that Mother wanted to go look at caskets. It didn't strike me as odd since she was in her mid-eighties, and I agreed to go along. At the funeral home (or *funelhome* as we say in Kentucky), we were shopping in the casket room with the funeral director, and Mother was saying that she liked this color but not that one, liked this lining but not that one, until she finally settled on her favorite. Then she said to me, "I want to make sure it has the *best* seal." So I asked the funeral director, "Can we have the *best* seal?"

"Oh, Mrs. Tucker, all the seals are the same," he replied. I looked at him with a *play along* nod and said again, "That's really great, but Mother wants the one with the *best* seal." I kind of tilted my head to the side until I got him to say, "Oh, yes. I'll make sure it has the *best* seal."

It dawned on me then to ask Mother, "Why is the seal important to you?" *Silly me*, I thought as she gave the obvious answer: "I don't want the bugs to get in." Okay. Got it. Bugs.

So the seal was decided. Next it was time for the vault. "I want the vault to be *super* sealed," she said. At this point I was trying not to smirk, and I thought, *Why? Do you not want to get out, or are you afraid somebody else might try to get in?*

"Mother, we're getting the *super* seal on the casket," I reminded her.

"Oh, no. We need the *super* seal for the vault so the snakes won't get in," she said, matter-of-factly. Snakes. So again I turned to the funeral director and asked, "Can you make sure the vault is *super* sealed so the snakes won't get in?"

By this time, he had caught my drift and smiled. "Yes, Mrs. Tucker, we'll make sure the vault gets the *super* seal, and then we'll add an *extra super seal* so the snakes won't get in."

Whew! We thanked him and walked toward the door as Mother peered over the edge of her casket one more time. "This doesn't look very comfortable does it?" she asked.

I laughed softly and said, "Mother, I really didn't know that comfort was an issue here."

"Oh, absolutely. I don't want to spend eternity lying here uncomfortable."

I stifled a laugh. "Mother, did you forget you're going to be dead? Uh, the body is broken, and you're not going to be there."

"Oh, that may be true, but just in case, I want a place that's really comfortable for me to spend the rest of my life since I'll be lying down. Oh, and make sure I have a bra and underwear and a slip if I wear a dress. I can go without shoes, even though you know how much I love my shoes."

I asked seriously, "Do you want to get in the casket and check out the comfort level?"

She looked at me like I was crazy and said, "Well, that's an odd suggestion."

It had become clear to me that she had very specific ideas of what she wanted for her funeral. We ended the day laughing about some of her wishes, and I felt secure that her funeral business was put to rest. But during another visit a few years later, as Mother approached her late eighties, she expressed that she wanted to "get my funeral outfit together." *No problem; how difficult could this be?* I thought.

Off to the department store we went, and she proceeded to select her outfit. Now, mind you, the lady helping us had no clue what the outfit was for. I stepped out to take a phone call while Mother was in the fitting room trying on clothes. When I returned, the saleslady was saying, "Oh, that's a beautiful color on you, but the sleeves need to be taken up, and the pants need to be hemmed."

I stopped her in midsentence. "Excuse me, Mother, would you cross your arms across your chest?" She complied, and I scrunched up her sleeves on both sides, looked at the legs, and said, "This will do fine. This will work really well."

The clerk looked at her and asked, "Where are you wearing this?"

"To a funeral," Mother replied.

"Whose funeral?"

Mother looked at me and then her and said, "My own."

The saleslady disappeared. We never saw her again, even when we were at checkout later. Meanwhile, my phone rang a second time, and when I returned to the fitting-room area, Mother was standing in front of the trifold mirror with my niece looking on. She was turned backside to the mirror, asking if the pants were too tight and if they made her hips look big. I cracked up! It was the funniest thing she had said yet.

"Mother, you're going to be dead. Are we burying you butt up? Are people going to kiss your butt on the way out? Because otherwise it really doesn't matter." We broke into such hard laughter that we almost peed ourselves right there in the fitting room of a major department store. We finally pulled ourselves together, and Mother paid for her very expensive outfit. (No slip needed, I might add.)

When it was time for Mother's funeral, we pulled out her new outfit and discovered that moths had eaten the pricey blouse she had bought to wear under the blazer even before she had passed away. I found a touch of humor in that and was reminded of that fun day.

She had asked me not to officiate at her funeral, but I did it anyway. I think she was worried about what I'd say. As I was speaking, I could hear her saying, "There you go again, using that voice you always used with me." I gave the sermon and spoke with pride and dignity to celebrate the life she had lived, even while knowing that we had had many struggles. As I finished, I could hear her saying, "Well, I asked you not to, and you did it anyway. Why am I surprised? You never did do what I told you to do."

We went to my brother's house after the funeral and had a wonderful day of family and fun, laughing and telling stories. Near the end, I announced to the few people left what a wonderful day it had been. My daughter, true to her blunt personality, said, "Yeah, except for the part where Grandma died."

And with that, we ended the day belly laughing to the point where we thought once again that we'd wet ourselves. (Are you seeing a trend?) When serious, life-altering events happen and we're trying to be reverent, respectful, and proper, the funniest things will happen. It's okay to laugh. Even death has humorous moments.

Allow the part of you that's been holding you back—the part that you've been holding on to so tightly—to die. Allow it to rest. Get a casket, seal it with the *best* seal, and then *super seal* it. Make sure that you put it in a place where you're comfortable with it staying. Dress it in nice clothes and send it to a vault. Put all your baggage in there and enter a new era of your life.

You've reframed, drawn new pictures, looked at the parts of yourself that were jaded, and dispelled those myths. You've diminished the too-serious side of yourself, lightened up, shed some moth-eaten old clothes, and donned some new ones. You've changed your Greek abbreviation to YTG and opened yourself up to trusting others, situations, and most importantly, yourself.

You've learned to stop judging and not be so fearful of the unknown, to live in the light instead of the dark. You've learned to let go of regrets and fix the things that needed fixing. You've come to terms with the fact that you're human, and that life will continue to throw challenges in your direction. Now close the lid on your baggage. It's time to take a new road on your journey.

Take your lists and index cards, and when you feel ready, put them in a pretty box and *super seal* it. Use Gorilla Glue or duct tape and put it in a safe place for comfort's sake. Don't throw it out—it is a part of you, and it's important to never forget what you've learned and how far you've come.

Once you've found its resting place, get out clean index cards and a special new box to keep them in, think of the plethora of opportunities ahead of you, and write the next chapter of your life. And please, keep laughing and loving.

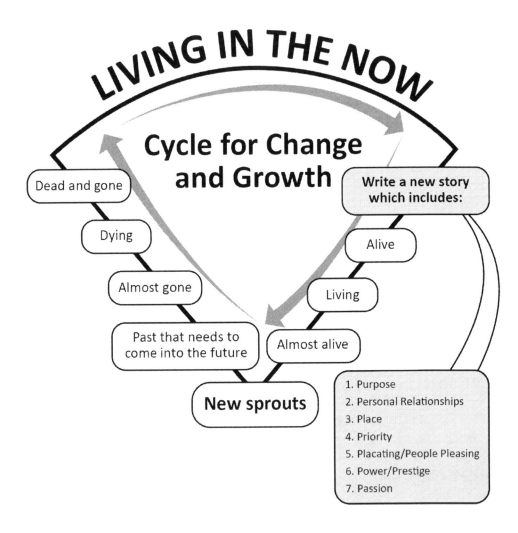

Not the End

Prescription for Mental Health
Summary of My Discoveries of Myself as I've Read This Book

Date begun:_____Date completed:_____

I chose to read this book because...

I was looking to find ways to change the following in myself:

The most significant things I've learned about myself as a result of reading this book and doing the exercises are...

I have recognized and am actively working toward changing the following self-defeating behavior patterns that have rendered me hopeless in the past:

Here's how I am putting these changes into practice:

The new decisions I have made about harmful early childhood experiences are...

The goals I have achieved are...

I have used the backward-planning process in these specific areas to achieve my goals:

My goals for today, three months, six months, one year, five years, and ten years from now are:
(Reminder: What I want in five to ten years is directly related to what I do today, and vice versa.)

Why do I want these goals, and are they clearly defined for success?

The life I visualize for myself now that I've made the above changes is...

What other issues would I like to deal with that maybe I skipped over and can reassess now?

Suggested Reading as You Continue on Your Journey

The Precious Present, by Spencer Johnson MD

Being Me, by Grady Nutt

The Shack, by William Paul Young

The Power of Positive Thinking, by Norman Vincent Peale

When the Heart Waits, by Sue Monk Kidd

Tracks of a Fellow Struggler, by John Claypool

> "Your individual journey is just beginning. Now is the time to experience value and hopefulness for the rest of your life."
> — *Cecilia Tucker*

About the Author

Cecilia Tucker, LMFT, is a well-respected marriage and family therapist in St. Petersburg, Florida. Now entering retirement, Cecilia has had a long career specializing in family therapy, adolescent issues, and grief counseling. Along with her thriving private practice, she was president and director of the Counseling Center for New Direction in St. Petersburg, served as a consultant to many national and international corporations, and hosted an acclaimed radio show that aired in half a dozen states featuring teenage guest speakers.

Before becoming a therapist, Cecilia earned a master's degree in religious education and social work from Southern Baptist Theological Seminary in 1979 and became the first woman in Florida to be ordained in the Southern Baptist Church. She is nationally recognized as a dynamic minister and public speaker renowned for her ability to tell it straight and make audiences laugh and cry. Topics of her public-speaking engagements include marriage, youth, parenting, and grief.

In addition to her family practice, Cecilia is a family law mediator, and an Approved Supervisor for the American Association of Marriage and Family Therapists. She is also a certified neurolinguistics programming practitioner.

For ten years Cecilia wrote a weekly column, "The Indomitable Teen" (IT), for the *St. Petersburg Times* (now the *Tampa Bay Times*).

Written in a teenager's voice, it addressed issues of eating disorders, peer pressure, sexuality, and adoption. Many of her articles have also been featured in the *St. Petersburg Times*, the *Kentucky New Era*, and the *Cherokee Scout*.

Cecilia developed and taught sex-ethics guidelines for several mainstream denominations and had a long, rewarding vocation as a minister in the greater St. Petersburg area. In 2011, due to her lack of proficiency with technological devices, she founded Gadg**it**Kids, a training service that employs young people ages eighteen to twenty-six to assist people of all ages in using their mobile devices. The employees bring their technological skills to the table, and Gadg**it**Kids trains them in interpersonal skills, learning styles, and business acumen.

Cecilia still resides in the St. Petersburg area with her husband of thirty-four years and enjoys time with her grown children and grandchildren. She finds inspiration when tucked away in her rustic mountain cabin in North Carolina.

As she eases into retirement, Cecilia has written *Who Needs a Damn Therapist, Anyway?* for people who feel they've lost hope but aren't sure where to turn, and for those who can't find the time for or afford a therapist. She's intertwined her own struggles and personal stories throughout each chapter, sharing of herself so that readers will feel encouraged to do the same. She wants readers to realize that just because she's a professional therapist, that doesn't mean she's immune to mistakes while managing life's trials. As she moves through her own life journey, she implements her training and experience to stay strong and be true to herself, and provide each reader with the same tools to move forward with a joyful life.

48560332R00077

Made in the USA
Charleston, SC
03 November 2015